THE ENCYCLOPEDIA
of Cut Flowers

THE ENCYCLOPEDIA
of Cut Flowers

What Flowers to Buy, When to Buy Them, and How to Keep Them Alive Longer

Calvert Crary

with Bruce Littlefield

BLACK DOG
& LEVENTHAL
PUBLISHERS
NEW YORK

Black Dog & Leventhal Publishers
Hachette Book Group
1290 Avenue of the Americas
New York, NY 10104

www.hachettebookgroup.com
www.blackdogandleventhal.com

First Edition: October 2023

Black Dog & Leventhal Publishers is an imprint of Perseus Books, LLC, a subsidiary of Hachette Book Group, Inc. The Black Dog & Leventhal Publishers name and logo are trademarks of Hachette Book Group, Inc.

The publisher is not responsible for websites (or their content) that are not owned by the publisher.

The Hachette Speakers Bureau provides a wide range of authors for speaking events.
To find out more, go to www.HachetteSpeakersBureau.com or email HachetteSpeakers@hbgusa.com.

Black Dog & Leventhal books may be purchased in bulk for business, educational, or promotional use. For more information, please contact your local bookseller or the Hachette Book Group Special Markets Department at Special.Markets@hbgusa.com.

Print book interior design by Katie Benezra

Library of Congress Cataloging-in-Publication Data
Names: Crary, Calvert, author. | Littlefield, Bruce (Bruce Duanne), author.
Title: The encyclopedia of cut flowers : what flowers to buy, when to buy them, and how to keep them alive for longer / Calvert Crary with Bruce Littlefield.
Description: First edition. | New York, NY : Black Dog & Leventhal Publishers/Hachette Book Group, 2023. | Includes index.
Summary: "From Calvert Crary, author of Flower School and executive director of FlowerSchool NY and FlowerSchool LA, The Encyclopedia of Cut Flowers is a first-of-its-kind, beautiful yet practical guide to buying and caring for 146 different varieties of cut flowers, including information on how to get the most for your money by prolonging the life of your flowers"—Provided by publisher.
Identifiers: LCCN 2022048101 (print) | LCCN 2022048102 (ebook) | ISBN 9780762483280 (trade paperback) | ISBN 9780762483297 (ebook)
Subjects: LCSH: Cut flowers—Encyclopedias. | Cut flowers—Postharvest technology—Encyclopedias.
Classification: LCC SB442.5 .C73 2023 (print) | LCC SB442.5 (ebook) | DDC 635.9/66—dc23/eng/20221118
LC record available at https://lccn.loc.gov/2022048101
LC ebook record available at https://lccn.loc.gov/2022048102

ISBNs: 978-0-7624-8328-0 (trade paperback), 978-0-7624-8329-7 (ebook)

Printed in China

1010

10 9 8 7 6 5 4 3 2 1

This book is dedicated to the amazing FlowerSchool students, community and flower lovers everywhere.

Introduction and Getting Started

THIS ISN'T A SELF-HELP BOOK, BUT IT COULD BE. Flowers have power. They have a life force. It has been scientifically proven that they make us undeniably happier. Research has shown they can also boost the creativity of an individual 45 percent, and studies have demonstrated they can reduce stress and anxiety.

Here in the fast-paced, pressure-filled twenty-first-century world, we can use all those things. As society runs amok around us, we seek out joy. Beautiful blooms—with their vibrant colors, their wonderful smells, and their perfect symmetry—offer us the gladness we long for. Flowers are healers.

You want proof? A study conducted by the Department of Horticulture at Kansas State University found that patients in hospital rooms decorated with flowers needed less postoperative pain medication, were less anxious and tired, had lowered systolic blood pressure rates, and were generally in a better psychological state than patients in rooms without flowers.

How do flowers do this for us? What about them makes them nature's pick-me-uppers? Let's get aesthetic. From the ever-popular rose to saucer-sized dahlias, flowers are eye-catching, beautiful, and unique. Some flowers are literally breathtaking because their fragrance captivates us, while others are delightful because of their vivid color or the inimitable ripple of their petals. Some flowers, like the peony, give us a few precious, fleeting moments, while astilbe's show goes on and on. Others, like the corpse plant, the largest flower in the world, only bloom every forty years. Some flowers capture our emotions by changing and developing over the course of several days, while others, like a chrysanthemum, are more like what you see is what you get.

Each flower is indeed its own special work of art, and this book is a brief visit to nature's most impressive and diverse art gallery. During this page-by-page garden tour of masterpieces—from agapanthus to zinnia—we'll identify, describe, and share tidbits of information on more than 140 of the most readily available cut flowers and some popular flowering branches. *The Encyclopedia of Cut Flowers* aims to help you also learn to care for these individual works of art. That way, even if your arrangement is in a simple bud vase, you will know the name of the flower and know how to make it last and show its best face.

On this gallery visit, you'll also learn to work with each specimen. There is, after all, a technique to doing flowers. It's both a meditation and a craft, and perhaps by the end of this book, flower-loving you will become floral artist you. Our hope is that this book will help you get maximum enjoyment out of the blooms in your own personal flower experience.

In this world of international shipping and specialized agricultural techniques, our appetite for the beauty of exotic flowers can be satisfied all year round with very few exceptions. Almost all flowers used in the cut flower trade are greenhouse grown. This controlled environment helps the grower protect the blooms from unstable weather, such as frost, rainstorms, and drought, and provides consistent light, which helps the flowers grow strong and blossom for their travel to your home. Additionally, two springs and two summers each year, one each in the northern and southern hemispheres, help ensure that most flowers are readily available regardless of the season you're in.

TRICKS USED BY FLORISTS

Doing flowers is a technique, a meditation, and a craft. To do them well, certain skills need to be mastered. But what does "doing it well" actually mean? The pinnacle to doing flowers well is making sure they all look healthy and blooming. Also, it's nice if they don't crash after the first day, but retire gracefully after several days of enjoyment.

All flowers are beautiful. For the purposes of this book, we hope to help you get maximum pleasure out of the flowers in your own personal daily flower regimen. Therefore, this book seeks to identify, describe, and impart tidbits about the most commonly available cut flowers and give you some ideas on how to work with specific flowers to make more florists out of us bloom lovers.

It is important to know that flowers are natural products and each flower is unique. Therefore, when we show you each flower, we intend to find the best likeness we can without overwhelming you with the tremendous number of choices that exists among each variety. For example, there are thousands of hybrid tea roses, but we show you only one variety and one color. There are thousands of tulip varieties, but we show you only a few. The hope is that you can find your favorites and learn some tricks to making them last and getting them beautifully arranged.

Fresh flowers should last a minimum of 5 days. No flower farmer or grower wants to invest in fields of flowers that only look good for 24 hours. If your flowers poop out early, there's likely another reason. Most probably, you acquired them already late in "vase life." If you're not cutting fresh out of your own garden, having a reputable supplier is key, one who cares for the flowers and will give you honest information about when they arrived. Another possibility is that the vase is filled with bacteria-laden water, which has been absorbed into the flower stem.

Let's start by talking about how to properly care for flowers. The word florists use for this is *conditioning*. All varieties of cut flowers must be conditioned properly to hydrate and finish their life cycle with dignity. There are several different levels of conditioning, but the general process is to get the flowers out of the transport stage, hydrate them, and make them ready to use in an arrangement. Flowers that have traveled for more than 2 hours out of water need time to hydrate and rest before using (like anyone who has traveled). Generally, for commercially cultivated cut flowers, we provide 2 to 6 hours of hydration before using them in an arrangement, because they are often coming off a plane flight. *All* flowers should be put in water that's been treated with antibacterial flower food or a hint of bleach to prevent bacteria growth.

From experience, we know that flowers that have been conditioned well are easier to add to bouquets and tend to fade more gracefully.

STRIPPING

Flowers that have not can more easily die and turn into a mountain of rotting plant matter in your vase.

Here are five essential tips for conditioning your flowers:

1. STRIPPING: Remove all or most of the foliage from the stem. Foliage will only cause the bloom to die, wilt, or, even worse, not to live up to its potential. Leaves have a way of sucking the hydration out of the stem and robbing the flower of life. When students ask to keep the foliage "because it's so pretty," our answer is always the same: No! It's better to remove it and replace it with a similar-looking foliage than to have the flower not live up to its potential.

The foliage from a flower can be removed in a variety of ways. Our favorite way is simply the finger strip. Hold the flower from the top of the stem with one hand and cup the stem with the other, then gently slide your hand down the stem to strip the foliage.

2. WATERING: We all know flowers need water, but one little-known fact is that water temperature can affect longevity significantly. Unfortunately for us, it can be hard to tell what works best with which flower. So, we go by general rules.

Flowers that have a soft stem, such as tulips and anemones, should get a fresh cut and be placed in cold water. This will help them hydrate but won't melt the stems.

Flower varieties that have hard or wooden stems, such as roses and lilacs, should be given a fresh cut and placed in hot water.

The rumor mill is filled with ideas on what to put in the vase to help flowers last longer, from adding vodka, Viagra, or aspirin to store-bought additives or flower foods. The main focus should in fact be keeping the water clean and clear of bacteria. (Hot water grows bacteria faster than cold.) We have found that changing the water regularly works very well, second only to the use of a light bleach solution or flower food. Traditional flower food powders are common and can be purchased almost anywhere. To make a bleach solution, mix a 10:1 ratio of water to bleach in a spray bottle and clearly mark it as your solution. Spray each vase three or four times before adding water and your flowers. Note that milkweeds should always be placed in hot water.

Water quality is super important. Most flower foods or water treatments for flowers are mainly antibacterials. Both flowers and humans need to drink clean, bacteria-free water. When you get your flowers home, pay special attention to the temperature of the conditioning water for your flowers. If a particular flower has special water recommendations, they'll be noted in the conditioning section of the entry. You may need hot (120–130°F), room temperature (50–60°F), and/or cold (35–40°F) water.

3. CUTTING: All flowers deserve a fresh cut immediately before placing in water. However, some can use a bit of extra work.

Most flowers benefit from a long cut with a floral knife. The standard method is cutting at a 45-degree angle, but professionals typically cut at a more severe angle to allow extra surface area to come into contact with the water and increase absorption. It's hard to remember which ones benefit, so best cut *all* flowers with a knife at an elongated angle. Flowers are generally thirsty.

Some flowers with woody stems, such as hydrangeas and lilacs, benefit from smashed and skinned stems. Don't go too crazy smashing. Do just enough to break or split 2 to 3 inches up the stem to increase surface area.

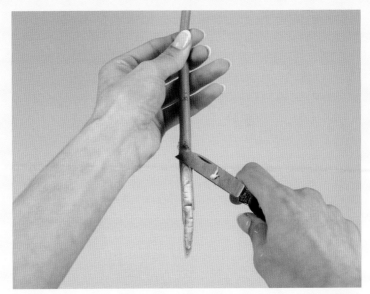

CUTTING

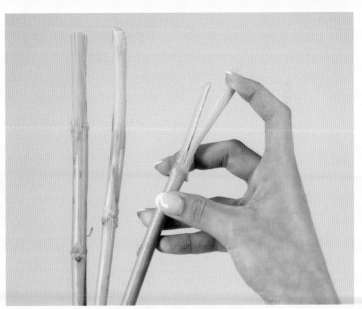

SMASHING

SPRAYING

4. SPRAYING: Some flowers like hydration from the top down rather than bottom up. Many varieties enjoy moist air and don't get enough from simply placing the stems in water. The two methods that florists use are spraying and coning. Spraying with water is exactly what it sounds like: fill a spray bottle with water and mist the flowers, both heads and stems. Be sure not to spray too much water on flowers, as that may trap water within the flower's petals, which promotes mold growth.

5. CONING: Wrapping a bunch of flowers in moist paper, such as kraft paper, will help them hydrate. First, remove the foliage (see stripping). Then, spray the paper you are using with a spray bottle of fresh water so that it is moist but not sopping wet. Lay the varieties in and close the cone around them. Give all of the stems a fresh cut so they are the same length (see photo above), put the bunch in the appropriate water temperature, and place the vase in a cooler or cool area for 4 to 6 hours.

6. STORING: Keeping flowers in a cool area is very helpful. We recommend something between 45 and 55°F. A refrigerator or well-air-conditioned room will do. Hydrating flowers is very similar to hydrating lettuce. After a good wash (spray), they need a spin (coning), and some time in the refrigerator. You know that will crisp lettuce right up. The same is true for your flowers.

TERMS USED FOR VARIETIES

Florists use several terms to describe the types of flowers. For example, the term *spray* means that the flower head might be smaller, but there will be multiple blooms on the stem. The most common will be the rose and the spray rose.

When flowers and foliage have more than one color, florists will say that they are *variegated*. This is more commonly associated with foliage, but you can also use the term to describe an unusual coloring on a standard variety.

SUPPLIES THAT ALL FLORISTS NEED

1. Florist knife and clipper. The tools that we find are best at FlowerSchool are the Victorinox floral knife and the clippers are the ARS 130DX pruning shears. Do not use imitations, as they are just not the same.

2. Vases for conditioning flowers. Tall, short, wide, and just plain big. Flowers come in all different shapes and sizes, so your vases should, too. We prefer glass in order to see what's happening in the water (bacteria growth or clear), and it just looks a whole lot nicer.

3. Small roll of kraft paper for coning flowers as well as covering your table for protection.

DESIGN TIPS

1. Use flowers that have the same shape. For example, linear flowers, such as calla lilies, tulips, and grasses, can easily go together. Flat flowers with a face, such as carnations, roses, and hydrangeas, go nicely together because they are all flat.

2. Use a single color. Pick one color and use multiple varieties of flowers all with the same color to make a bold statement.

3. Use the classic method of mixing colors for bouquets with more than one color: 65 percent primary color, 25 percent a shade of the primary color, and 10 percent a complementary color.

4. Surprise your viewer with something unexpected. For example, try adding a non-floral element, like tomatoes or grapes on the vine, a dried flower that's been painted, or some other unexpected color. Nothing is out of bounds here.

There are obvious exceptions to every rule, but these will give you a base to work from. Use these tips to get the buying (or cutting) started!

—

The Encyclopedia of Cut Flowers aims to help budding florists identify and care for many popular cut flower varieties. At the very least, you will know the names of the flowers and how to make them last and last and last some more.

The Flowers

Agapanthus

(Lily of the Nile, African Lily)

More than six hundred cultivars and hybrids of agapanthus exist. Shades of blue are the most familiar, but lilac, pink, and white are also available.

AVAILABILITY
Early spring through late summer

CONDITIONING TIPS
Agapanthus stems can range from just 8 inches to up to 6 feet, and each stalk displays its own little globe-shaped cluster of flowers. When buying them, look for blooms that are just beginning to open. Cut at a 45-degree angle with a sharp knife and place in hot water. Agapanthus is sensitive to ethylene, so keep them away from ripening fruit.

FASCINATING FACTS
The name agapanthus is derived from the Greek words *agape* (love) and *anthos* (flower). Given the meaning of its name, agapanthus is often used to symbolize love, and its flowers were once worn by women to encourage fertility and excellent health during pregnancy. This tropical beauty is a member of the garlic family, and with its strong line and romantic appeal, it makes for a theatrical display.

Alchemilla

(Lady's Mantle, Lion's Foot, Bear's Foot, Nine Hooks)

Prized for its foliage, lady's mantle has round, emerald green leaves with scalloped edges and small clusters of tiny chartreuse flowers, which make a beautiful bouquet filler.

AVAILABILITY
Spring and summer

CONDITIONING TIPS
Choose flowers that are yellow with no brown. Cut the stems and place them in warm water. In a vase, they like to stay cool. Lady's mantle pairs well with almost all colors, but it's really great with purple and pink. It also dries well. Simply bundle the stems and hang them upside down in a cool, ventilated spot until dry. They last longer than many dried flowers.

FASCINATING FACTS
Lady's mantle pumps water from the earth, which then comes out of tiny holes located in the teeth of the leaves. In the Middle Ages, alchemists believed that water to be "the fifth element"—the ultimate water of life, which would give eternal youth to the person drinking it. Cheers to that!

Allium

(Ornamental Onion, Wild Garlic, Chive)

The color range of allium flowers is considerable. Most popular range from deep purple to white. There is a selection of late spring varieties that aren't globe-shaped but rather are cupped and have a large range of colors from orange, red, and purple to white.

AVAILABILITY

Spring to September

CONDITIONING TIPS

Allium should be harvested when the flower is about half open. As soon as you cut a stem, you'll realize that alliums are members of the onion family. Alliums will make the water smell a little like onion soup, so the water should be changed daily. Clean water is key to long vase life for alliums, which can range from 10 to 21 days. The flower heads of alliums can be dried, too.

FASCINATING FACTS

An allium flower head is a pom-pom-shaped cluster of individual florets and resembles a firework explosion. They can be almost 6 feet tall and 6 inches in diameter. Allium symbolizes good fortune, unity, patience, and humility.

Alstroemeria

(Peruvian Lily, Parrot Lily, Lily of the Incas)

Alstroemerias resemble miniature lilies. The brightly colored flowers are shaped like trumpets and come in many shades of red, orange, purple, green, and white. They are often flecked with spots or striped and streaked with a darker color. The "upside-down" leaves are variable in shape, and the blades have smooth edges. Alstroemerias have no fragrance.

AVAILABILITY
All year

CONDITIONING TIPS
Recut the stems at an angle and remove the leaves. Fill a clean vase with cool water and add flower food. Change the water every 3 days or so, trimming the stems each time. Display alstroemerias in a cool, shady spot, avoiding proximity to ripening fruit. Vase life is up to 14 days.

FASCINATING FACTS
Alstroemeria is known as the friendship flower, and since it has no fragrance, it would be great for friends who have pollen allergies.

Amaranthus

(Tassel Flower, Love-Lies-Bleeding, Cat's Tail,
Velvet Flower, Foxtail)

Amaranthus comes in a variety of forms and textures, from plumy flower
stalks to cascading hanging ropes, and a range of colors, including red,
burgundy, orange-brown, yellow, and green. Its foliage can be rather
dramatic in red and yellow.

AVAILABILITY
Summer to fall

CONDITIONING TIPS
Amaranthuses drink a lot of water, so keep them well watered and mist
them often with a spray bottle. They will last nicely in a vase for 5 days
or so. Amaranthuses are also easy to dry and, as long as they're kept out of
direct sunlight, will retain their color.

FASCINATING FACTS
A native of South America, amaranthus gets its name from the Greek
amarantos, which means "unfading." True to their name, the plants
keep their deep red, green, or yellow blooms vibrant for a long time.
Amaranthus can add some nice drama to arrangements.

Amaranthus Spike

Amaryllis

(Easter Lily, Jersey Lily, Naked Lily)

There are many amaryllis varieties to choose from. Flowers range from 4 to 10 inches in size and can range from single blooms to a cluster of four per stem. Some specialty varieties have double blooms—a bloom within a bloom. While the most popular colors are red and white, flowers may also be pink, salmon, apricot, rose, or deep burgundy. Around the holidays, red and white ones make merry decorations.

AVAILABILITY
This bulb flower blooms in the early spring, but is often forced in greenhouses to be available in early winter.

CONDITIONING TIPS
Amaryllis flowers actually last longer when cut and put in a vase. The best time to cut the flower is right before the bud opens. With a sharp knife, cut the plant at a 45-degree angle 1 inch or so above the neck of the bulb and place in a super clean vase of water. Stems will often split and curl at the base in water, so designers typically use a rubber band or waterproof tape around the base of the stem to prevent this. If you change the water often, they can look gorgeous for 14 days or more. Since the stems are hollow and the flower is heavy when fully bloomed, insert a 20- to 24-inch-long straw, bamboo cane, or stick into the stem to offer support and prevent the stem from breaking.

FASCINATING FACTS
Each year, more than 10 million amaryllis bulbs are sold in the US alone. The Netherlands is the world leader in amaryllis exports and offers the widest range of varieties and highest quality. Amaryllis flowers are the symbol of the desire to be loved, which makes them excellent for the holiday season.

Anemone

(Wind Flower, Lily of the Field, Poppy Anemone)

These flowers come in a wide assortment of forms, from single to double bloom, and a rainbow of colors, including white, yellow, rose, blue, purple, pink, scarlet, rust, coral, and copper. A variety known as Japanese anemone, which blooms in the fall, has smaller flower petals than common anemone. The most sought after are the white/blush flowers with a black center.

AVAILABILITY
Common anemone: winter to spring; Japanese anemone: fall

CONDITIONING TIPS
Anemones have a long vase life as long as you get them fresh, so buy them when they are no more than half open. The telltale sign of freshness is how close the flower is to the frilled green skirt on the stem beneath the flower. If the skirt is ½ inch from the flower, they will tend to be fresh. If the flower has grown more than 1 inch above the skirt, they probably have been sitting around for a while. Note that anemones are heavy drinkers, so change and refill their water often. Anemones are phototropic and will open and close when exposed to light and heat, so keep that in mind when using them in an arrangement.

FASCINATING FACTS
Anemones are often depicted alongside the Virgin Mary as she mourns the death of Christ. The red anemones in these paintings are said to symbolize Christ's blood. Anemones close at night and open in the morning and thus serve as a reminder to enjoy the moment.

Anthurium

(Flamingo Flower, Painted Tongue, Tail Flower)

Anthuriums are available mainly in shades of red, but also in an array of nice colors, including green, pink, white, and chocolate.

AVAILABILITY
All year, but best in summer

CONDITIONING TIPS
Cut 1 inch or so off the end of the stem and put it in a clean vase with fresh water. Changing the water once a week and cutting off ¼ inch of the stem will keep the bloom looking good for 14 days or more.

FASCINATING FACTS
The anthurium "flower" is actually a heart-shaped spathe, which is a waxy, modified leaf that flares from the base of a spike where the real (tiny) flowers grow. Its name is derived from the Greek words *anthos* and *oura*, which translates to "flowering tail." Because it looks nothing like other flowers, its exotic beauty can sometimes be used in more interesting ways, from being painted to giving a playful Dr. Seuss–like quality to an arrangement. Anthuriums are symbolic of great ambition, happiness, and hospitality.

Asclepias

(Butterfly Weed, Swamp Milkweed)

There are several different varieties of asclepias that all have a different coloring. The orange variety with red dots is the most common, but asclepias can also be found in white, pink, lavender, yellow, and red.

AVAILABILITY
Late spring and early summer

CONDITIONING TIPS
Stems should be cut when more than half the flowers are open, as buds do not open well once the stem is cut. These interesting mini-star flowers are a milkweed, so when you remove the foliage, you will see a sticky white substance ooze from the stem; this is how the plant drinks. Hydrate asclepias stems with hot water after giving them a fresh cut. Don't mix them with other flowers until they have been drained of their sap.

FASCINATING FACTS
Asclepias plants are known to be butterfly magnets and have a medicinal history as a treatment for pleurisy, a wheezing, coughing ailment that was common during early colonial times. *Asclepias tuberosa* was so effective in treating this ailment it earned the common name pleurisy root.

Aspidistra

(Cast-iron Plant, Barroom Plant, Butcher's Plant)

Aspidistras are lance-shaped green leaves with variegation. They are approximately 15 to 18 inches high and 3 to 6 inches wide.

AVAILABILITY
All year

CONDITIONING TIPS
Aspidistra leaves are popular greenery for centerpieces and wedding decor because the leaves can be cut, folded, and twisted and will keep nicely for weeks. You'll also see these leaves lining the insides of glass vases to conceal untidy stems.

FASCINATING FACTS
In Victorian England, aspidistra plants became hugely popular, and its ability to tolerate neglect as a houseplant got it dubbed the cast-iron plant. In Holland, this hardiness for thriving in low temperatures and little sunlight helped it become known as the butcher's plant.

Asplenium, Crispy Wave

(Nest Fern)

Crispy wave asplenium can be recognized by its fresh green upright leaves featuring ruffles on the edges.

AVAILABILITY
All year

CONDITIONING TIPS
This interesting-looking fern leaf can last for weeks if hydrated. It should be rigid like a hardy piece of kale. If the leaf begins to wilt, then submerge the entire leaf in a dish of cold water until it is rehydrated.

FASCINATING FACTS
The botanic name *Asplenium* comes from the Greek word *asplenon*, which translates to "spleen herb." During the Middle Ages, the fern was used as a medicine against spleen diseases. This fern is also available as a houseplant, and while it is a nice addition to a home florist's cutting garden, it also provides extra oxygen and removes all sorts of harmful substances from the air.

Aster, China

(Annual Aster)

China asters are known for their bright purple, pink, red, or white coloring with classic yellow centers. Their oval foliage is green with toothy edges. Unlike other aster varieties, this one is special because it is an annual and not a perennial.

AVAILABILITY
Late summer to early fall

CONDITIONING TIPS
Do not put foliage in the water, as it rots and decreases vase life. Change the water every few days and the flowers will have a vase life of 7 to 14 days.

FASCINATING FACTS
Asters are supposedly great meteorologists. Closed petals on asters predict rain in the forecast. In ancient times, it was believed that magical fairies slept beneath aster petals when they closed at sunset.

Astilbe

(False Goat's Beard)

Astilbe produces an attractive mound of glossy, fernlike foliage with delicate feather-like plumes of colorful flowers that tend to be light in coloring from white to blush to pink. There is also a less common light burgundy color.

AVAILABILITY
Early spring to summer

CONDITIONING TIPS
Astilbes make great filler flowers to add texture and a delicate touch to arrangements. To ensure the longest vase life, the top half of the flowers should have swollen buds before being harvested.

FASCINATING FACTS
Astilbe flowers are long blooming and a symbol of commitment to someone you care about. When you give someone astilbes, it's a promise of forever dedication.

Astrantia

(Masterwort, Hattie's Pincushion)

These long-lasting, star-shaped flower heads have five petals and come in a variety of colors, including white, pink, and red.

AVAILABILITY
Summer

CONDITIONING TIPS
The hollow stems of astrantias love hot water. If they look droopy, give them a fresh cut, remove the foliage, place the stems in a vase of hot water, mist the tops with a spray bottle of water, and place the vase in a refrigerator. They will pop right back.

FASCINATING FACTS
Astrantias are light and have very nice movement. They are just as beautiful in a bouquet as they are in the garden. Astrantias have rigid stems and flowers that retain their color and shape, and they make great dried flowers. They symbolize strength, courage, and protection.

Banksia

(Australian wildflower)

There are more than 170 species of this native Australian wildflower, which produces elongated, cone-shaped spikes. Colors include gold, silver, yellow, green, and violet. Some species have multicolored spikes.

AVAILABILITY
Late summer to fall

CONDITIONING TIPS
These desert flowers are as hardy as anything available and can keep for many weeks when simply placed in water. For extra longevity and to keep the foliage hydrated, the flowers should be stored in a damp cone (see introduction for more information on coning).

FASCINATING FACTS
The spike is not just one flower but is made up of hundreds, sometimes thousands, of tiny flowers.

Bouvardia

(Firecracker Bush, Trumpetellia, Hummingbird Flower)

The dainty jasmine-like flowers of bouvardias can be single or double blooms in beautiful little clusters. They are available in white, red, and all colors in between.

AVAILABILITY
Early spring through late fall

CONDITIONING TIPS
Bouvardias make excellent cut flowers and can last up to 20 days in a vase. They can be used as either filler or accent flowers. To extend the life of the flowers, remove excess foliage and the top bud.

FASCINATING FACTS
Bouvardias are related to gardenias and are often used in celebration bouquets because they are said to represent enthusiasm. They make a great gift for people who have a zest for life.

Bruniaceae

(Berzelia, Brunia, Button Bush, Snow Bush)

The whimsical flowers of the bruniaceae family, a cluster of knobby fruiting heads on a long, woody stalk with feathery leaves, look otherworldly. These shrubs have needlelike leaves and adorable tiny button-like flower heads, which add great texture to design. Varieties include green, red, and silver, making them ideal for winter white arrangements.

AVAILABILITY
Most of the year; peak: summer into late fall

CONDITIONING TIPS
If you can, buy them before the flowers are open because branches with cones last longer than those that have already open flowers. Leaves should be glossy green, and the flowers shouldn't have brown spots. Avoid bunches if the leaves have yellowed. Use a half cap (about a quarter teaspoon) of bleach in the vase, and these can last 14 days or more.

FASCINATING FACTS
Brunia berries aren't actually berries, but ball-shaped flowers. The brunia shrub is native to South Africa and can grow more than 6 feet tall. Its deep green foliage looks prickly, like that of a pine tree.

Bupleurum

(Hare's-ear, Thoroughwax)

This flower is closer to field foliage than a flower and is popular due to its light green coloring. Bupleurum can grow up to 3 feet tall.

AVAILABILITY
Spring into summer

CONDITIONING TIPS
Pick strong stems with bright green foliage and colorful, well-spread-out blooms that are already more than half fully blossomed. Use caution when pulling stems apart because they tend to tangle. Turn them upside down and shake gently to loosen. Bupleurums need hot water and mist to hydrate fully.

FASCINATING FACTS
Bupleurums are closely related to fennel and dill. The Chinese name for them, *chai hu*, translates to "kindling for the barbarians." They have been used in Chinese medicine for thousands of years as a remedy for fevers, fatigue, respiratory infections, and digestive issues.

Calathea

Calatheas have large green and white leaves with a bold, contrasting purple on the backside.

AVAILABILITY
All year

CONDITIONING TIPS
Tropical leaves like calathea are very wide (up to 6 inches) all the way down the stem. The common thinking that foliage should never be in water is tossed out the window here. These tropical leaves are often used to line the inside of a glass vase as an accent. Tropical foliage, including the calathea leaf, don't break down quickly and will do just fine in water.

FASCINATING FACTS
These leaves have a nice personality and can offer a chic accent in unconventional arrangements. They can also be used for tabletop decor, flat and without water. In this capacity, they last only a few hours.

Calendula

(Pot Marigold)

Calendula has bright yellow or orange daisy-like blossoms.

AVAILABILITY
Early to late summer

CONDITIONING TIPS
Some people find the long, narrow, and hairy leaves of calendula to be stinky, but they make great, long-lasting cut flowers. When cut, calendula oozes a sticky resinous sap. Put them in a vase with hot water.

FASCINATING FACTS
Edible calendula flowers have a slightly peppery taste. They can be eaten raw or cooked or used to liven up a cocktail. Calendula is often referred to as poor man's saffron because it can be used as a substitute for more expensive saffron. People make tea and tinctures out of calendula, as it is said to help boost the immune system.

Calla Lily
(*Zantedeschia*)

Calla lilies come in just about every color but vary widely in size.
The standard ones are 12 to 18 inches high, but one variety known as
"Colombe de la Paix" reaches almost 3 feet.

AVAILABILITY
All year; best from early spring to mid-summer

CONDITIONING TIPS
Calla lily stems are soft and fragile. To keep the stems from rotting, it's best
to put them in a tall vase with only 1 inch of treated water. You can tell if
the flowers are old if they are shriveled. If this is the case, don't buy them;
they are dehydrated beyond repair and will not come back.

FASCINATING FACTS
This flower is considered a line flower, best used in long, tall arrangements
where negative space is valued. The foliage also makes a great material, so
if you can cut from your garden, you get the added bonus of the foliage.

Campanula

(Venus Looking Glass, Bellflower, Rampion, Rapunzel)

Tubular, bell-shaped campanula flowers are loosely clustered and come in pink, white, purple, lavender, and blush.

AVAILABILITY
Spring

CONDITIONING TIPS
Cut the stems ½ inch from the bottom and place them in hot water. Remove the foliage and give them a spritz of cool water. Hydrate for 2 hours before using in an arrangement.

FASCINATING FACTS
Campanula is Latin for "bell." In 1812, the Brothers Grimm used Rapunzel for their princess's name because Rapunzel, or *Campanula rapunculus*, was familiar to readers of the time; it was a common herb, which Rapunzel's mother stole from the witch's garden.

Celosia, Brain Flower

(Plumed, Cockscomb)

The brain flower variety of celosia resembles the wavy folds of the brain. Celosias are firm to the touch and have a velvety look and feel. They come in a variety of colors, including red, orange, and yellow.

AVAILABILITY
Summer

CONDITIONING TIPS
The celosia stem is quite soft; it is best to put it in a vase of cool water to prevent it from breaking down. Change the water often with this flower, every 2 days, and it will last up to 14 days in a vase.

FASCINATING FACTS
Cockscomb is symbolic of the expression of eternal love and that true love will last forever.

Celosia, Spiked

(Woolflower)

Spiked celosia and plumed celosia heads are pointed and feathery and come in a variety of colors, including red, orange, and yellow.

AVAILABILITY
Summer

CONDITIONING TIPS
The celosia stem is quite soft; it is best to put it in a vase of cool water to prevent it from breaking down. Celosia plants generally make great cut flowers because they last a long time in an arrangement.

FASCINATING FACTS
The leaves of celosia are edible and taste like spinach. Celosia is often used medicinally to treat blood diseases, mouth and eye problems, and intestinal worms. The flowers help treat diarrhea, and the seeds can be used to treat chest problems. Consult a doctor before eating your arrangement.

Cherry Blossom (*Prunus* spp.)

(Sakura, Japanese Cherry, Yoshino Cherry)

The classic pink cherry blossom is known as sakura or Japanese cherry. The popular white variety is known as Yoshino cherry.

AVAILABILITY
Spring, for just 7 or 14 days

CONDITIONING TIPS
Split the woody stems at the bottom by cutting up the stem 1 inch, and then put them in hot water to help force the flowers to open. Once open, mist the flowers to help keep them attached to the branch.

FASCINATING FACTS
More than 1.5 million visitors go to Washington, DC, each year to see the annual cherry blossom bloom. The Japanese have long celebrated cherry blossoms as a symbol of renewal and the brevity and beauty of life. During the blossoming, they go all out with outdoor parties of family and friends called *hanami*, which means "watching blossoms."

Chrysanthemum, Cremon

(Dutch Football Mum)

The cremon mum is known for its long, soft, round flower petals and long vase life. This is a Dutch variety that is a relative of the popular football mum, which has become hard to get, and a good replacement. Another variation is the spider mum, which has longer flower petals that vary in length and curl at the ends.

AVAILABILITY
All year; especially popular in the fall

CONDITIONING TIPS
The chrysanthemum is one of the longest-lasting cut flowers, lasting well over 14 days. Make sure all the leaves are removed before putting them in a vase. Chrysanthemums give off a large amount of ethylene gas, so keep them away from ethylene-sensitive flowers, like orchids and carnations.

FASCINATING FACTS
Fifteen percent of all cut flowers sold in the world are chrysanthemums.

Chrysanthemum, Spider Mum

The spider mum is a somewhat groovy member of the chrysanthemum family and gets its common name from its long, narrow petals, which resemble a spider's legs. Spider mums come in a vast array of shapes, sizes, and colors, including white, yellow, orange, red, pink, and lavender.

AVAILABILITY
All year

CONDITIONING TIPS
Spider mums are long lasting; just remove the leaves to avoid yellowing and cut the stems at an angle to ensure the flowers get enough water to drink. A few drops of bleach in room temperature water keeps them from getting funky. Keep the ends trimmed and the water fresh, and spider mums will last around 14 days in a vase.

FASCINATING FACTS
In Asia, the mum is a symbol of a long and happy life.

Chrysanthemum, Spray

(Pom-pom Chrysanthemum, Button Mum)

The flowers of the button mum tend to be open and small, and their tightly packed petals create miniature pom-pom blooms. Thousands of colors are available, but spray mums are typically found mostly in primary and secondary colors, like red, yellow, white, or green.

AVAILABILITY
All year; especially popular in the fall

CONDITIONING TIPS
The chrysanthemum is one of the longest-lasting cut flowers, lasting well over 14 days. Make sure all the leaves are removed before putting them in a vase. Chrysanthemums give off a large amount of ethylene gas, so keep them away from ethylene-sensitive flowers, like orchids and carnations.

FASCINATING FACTS
Chrysanthemum leaves and flowers are edible. In Chinese cuisine, the leaves are steamed or boiled and eaten as leafy vegetables. Chrysanthemum tea is also a popular tasty drink in China, with many health benefits.

Clematis

(Old Man's Beard)

Whimsical clematis, with its starlike flowers, comes in varying shades of purple and brilliant white as well as pink, red, and blue. Some growers are cultivating doubles, meaning that there are more than five flower petals.

AVAILABILITY
Summer

CONDITIONING TIPS
Clematis vines make excellent cut flowers and can last 10 or more days as long as you cut with a sharp knife and put the stems in a vase of hot water. The blooms should be about half open, and the stamens should be held together and not unfolding. Fully open blooms can be cut; they just won't last as long. For a special event, blooms at various stages give arrangements a natural look. If you find that your clematis blooms are drooping, revive them by recutting the stems and giving the flower a spritz of water.

FASCINATING FACTS
Clematis vines are flexible and quite durable, so they are great in hand-tied bouquets and wreaths. The woody stems contain large vessels, which allow air to pass through them. It was once a pastime to break off pieces of the stem and smoke it like a cigar.

Columbine (*Aquilegia* spp.)

(Granny's Bonnet)

Columbines are known for their five-petaled flowers, which have long, brightly colored, backward-extending spurs that are pouch-like and contain nectar. There are more than seventy different species of this perennial, which comes in a variety of colors and can be commonly found in fields at higher altitudes in early spring.

AVAILABILITY
Spring

CONDITIONING TIPS
Remove the foliage, give the stem a fresh cut, and put it into hot water. These flowers also like a mist.

FASCINATING FACTS
Columbine comes from the Latin word *columba*, which means "dove."

Coreopsis

(Tickseed)

With their bright and happy little blossoms and long, wiry stems, coreopsis plants have great charm. Although typically yellow, these flowers come in different colors, including red, orange, maroon, and lavender, and some are bicolored. Their common name, tickseed, refers to the fact that one end of the coreopsis seed is spiny and the other end looks like a tiny head, making the seeds look like a collection of parasitic ticks. Coreopsis foliage has an herbal fragrance somewhat like that of dill.

AVAILABILITY
Late spring through early fall

CONDITIONING TIPS
Coreopsis is a terrific cut flower, very sunny and summery with a wildflower feel. All foliage below the waterline and most above should be removed to extend vase life. Cut the stems under running water on the diagonal to prevent air bubbles and submerge them in lukewarm water for a couple hours or overnight.

FASCINATING FACTS
Native Americans boiled coreopsis flowers into teas and used the plant to treat rheumatism, diarrhea, and abdominal pain. It was believed that coreopsis would protect a person from being hit by lightning. Coreopsis has also been used as an insect repellant. European settlers to North America stuffed their mattresses with dried coreopsis to repel bedbugs.

Coriander
(Coriandrum sativum)

(Confetti Flower, Cilantro)

The flowers on coriander plants are quite sweet, with white or very pale pink petals. Admittedly, coriander is more popular as an herb than a flower, but its flowers are light and airy, which makes it perfect for whimsical flower arrangements.

AVAILABILITY
Summer

CONDITIONING TIPS
Remove all the foliage, cut the stems on an angle, spritz the flowers with water, and place in hot water.

FASCINATING FACTS
Coriander is a widely used herb around the world. Besides being tasty in guacamole, coriander can be used to regulate elevated blood sugar levels in people with diabetes and helps with digestive problems. Coriander has also been used to treat high cholesterol, mouth ulcers, painful joints, and even hemorrhoids.

Cornflower
(*Centaurea cyanus*)

(Bachelor's Button)

Cornflowers are available in various shades of blue, maroon, pink, red, purple, and white. All the colors, besides blue, were created by selective breeding. Cornflowers can produce both single and double blooms.

AVAILABILITY
Summer

CONDITIONING TIPS
Cornflowers have a vase life of about 10 days as long as all the foliage is removed. Because it is a field flower, you may want to change the water often as it begins to smell quickly.

FASCINATING FACTS
Cornflower is so named because it often grows wild in fields of corn. The nickname bachelor's button comes from the old practice of men wearing a cornflower in the buttonhole of their suit when they are in love or ready to be.

Cotinus

(Smoke Bush, Smoke Tree, Cloud Tree, Wig Tree)

Smoke bush leaves range from purple to maroon to green. In late spring, textured purply-pink puffs that look like smoke start to bloom on the tips of branches.

AVAILABILITY
Summer to early fall

CONDITIONING TIPS
Smoke bush is drought tolerant and can remain looking great out of water for many hours. If left alone, the smoke bush flower will become a dried flower (resembling a tumbleweed), and you can even spray-paint it.

FASCINATING FACTS
Smoke bush leaves have red veins at the edges. When crushed, they smell like orange peel. The plumes are a great choice for large-scale displays and creating flower clouds. They have become a popular design choice for weddings.

Craspedia

(Billy Button, Billy Ball, Woolyhead, Golden Drumstick)

The notable characteristic of this quirky flower is the vibrant, ball-shaped clusters that form at the top of each stem, which are made up of tiny, symmetrically arranged florets. The yellow balls are a favorite among florists for adding a playful texture and a happy color to arrangements.

AVAILABILITY
Summer

CONDITIONING TIPS
Craspedia is virtually the same dried or fresh, so, when the price is right, be sure to get a nice quantity for reserve. There is no need to hydrate this flower, as it is basically dried on arrival. Many designers paint them different colors to add interest.

FASCINATING FACTS
Craspedia's globe-shaped flower heads, which can reach the size of a tennis ball, are mathematical perfection. Its tiny florets arranged within each sphere mimic a perfect Fibonacci spiral.

Curly Willow
(*Salix matsudana*)

(Peking Willow, Corkscrew Willow)

Curly willow trees produce unusual twisted and twirled branches. The foliage is green in summer and yellow in the fall.

AVAILABILITY
All year

CONDITIONING TIPS
Recut stems underwater and place in a vase with a capful (about a quarter teaspoon) of household bleach. The curls are so charming that its branches can stand alone in a vase. It can be used fresh or dried.

FASCINATING FACTS
Salicylic acid is found in the bark of the curly willow, and prior to the development of aspirin, it was long used as a pain and fever reliever.

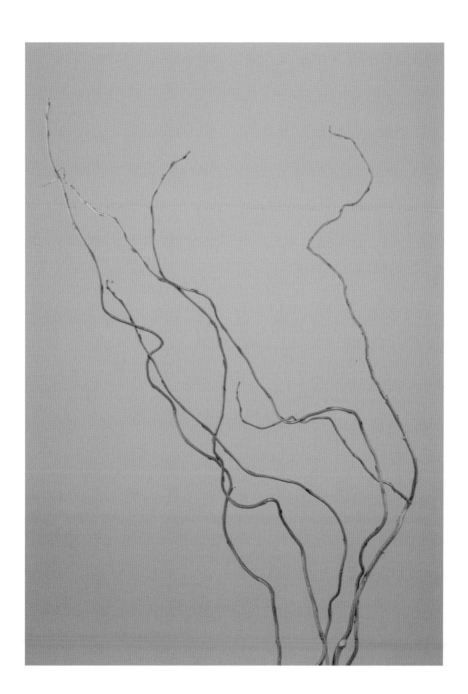

Dahlia, Standard

Dahlias come in a wide range of colors and textures. In fact, there are more than sixty thousand named varieties of this garden favorite. There's every color imaginable, including red, purple, orange, yellow, white, coral, and pink.

AVAILABILITY
Late summer to first frost

CONDITIONING TIPS
Dahlias like cool weather and cold water. Cut the stems with a knife and place them in cold water with antibacterials. Dahlia petals tend to wilt pretty quickly. It's best to spritz the flower directly with water to keep it hydrated.

FASCINATING FACTS
Dahlias can be found in every color except blue, and yes, breeders are working on trying to create a blue-blooming dahlia. These flowers often show their faces on a 90-degree angle, which can make them hard to work with. So, when making a mixed arrangement, put the dahlias in last.

Dahlia, Café au Lait

Dahlias come in a rainbow of colors and varieties. Café au lait dahlias are given the nickname dinner plate, since they can be 10 inches in diameter.

AVAILABILITY
Late summer to first frost

CONDITIONING TIPS
Be aware that this variety of dahlia only lasts 2 or 3 days, and once the weather is too hot, it will fall apart.

FASCINATING FACTS
The Café au Lait dahlia is most prized when oversized. It can get extremely big. Other varieties that can get big are Spartan and labyrinth.

Dahlia, Curved Petal

(Pom-pom Dahlia)

Color isn't the only characteristic that makes dahlias different from one another—dahlias grow in a range of shapes, too. Pom-pom dahlias have curved petals and grow in a rounded shape.

AVAILABILITY
Late summer to first frost

CONDITIONING TIPS
Dahlias like cool weather and cold water. Cut with a knife and place stems in cold water with antibacterials. Dahlia petals tend to wilt pretty quickly. It is best to spritz the flower directly with water to keep it hydrated.

FASCINATING FACTS
The dahlia is the national flower of Mexico. The mountains of Mexico and Guatemala are considered the originating spot for today's dahlias. In the sixteenth century, Spanish conquistadors gathered dahlia bulbs to bring home.

Daisy, Gerber
(*Gerbera* spp.)

This flat flower has more varieties than most other cut flowers, with centers ranging from white to green to brown to black and flower petals in various hues of white, red, orange, yellow, pink, lilac, purple, and bicolor—but not blue. If it's blue, it's artificial! Additionally, the petals themselves can be flat or curled. The gerbera flower is actually a cluster of hundreds of individual little flowers.

AVAILABILITY
Year round

CONDITIONING TIPS
Gerbera daisies are famous for their slender stems, which can be an issue when designing because they flop over and break easily. If it comes wearing a support straw around its stem, you should leave it on. If there is no straw, the stems can be wired to stay upright. Gerberas have a vase life of up to 14 days.

FASCINATING FACTS
You might want to place a vase of gerberas by your bed at night to get better sleep. Gerberas inhale carbon dioxide and exhale oxygen at night, unlike most other flowers, which do that during the day.

Delphinium

Delphiniums are tall—they can grow up to 3 feet high! The flowers look like spurs and come in a variety of colors, including pink, blue, periwinkle, purple, and white. It has become one of the top-selling florist flowers in the world because it is one of the few large flowers that are naturally blue. It was used by Native Americans to make blue dye.

AVAILABILITY
Early spring to early summer

CONDITIONING TIPS
Select stems with one-third or more of the flowers in bloom. Delphiniums have hollow stems like a drinking straw, so recut the stems with a knife, put them in hot water, and mist the flowers with a spray bottle of water. Add a drop of bleach to the vessel to keep the stems from getting slimy and contaminating the water. Delphiniums will last up to 7 days.

FASCINATING FACTS
In ancient times, delphiniums were used to repel scorpions, lice, and other parasites and were thought to protect against lightning, eye diseases, and even witches. Delphiniums are poisonous to both humans and animals, because they secrete the alkaloid delphinine, which can lead to severe illness, paralysis, and death from respiratory failure—so be sure to wash your hands after handling.

Dense, Blazing Star (*Liatris spicata*)

(Blazing Star, Gayfeather)

The blazing star gets its name because of the tall, brilliant blooms that appear on a spike and look like bottle brushes. Linear, grasslike leaves are clumped toward the base of the plant but extend up the stem toward the showy tufted flower cluster. Unlike most flowers, they bloom from the top down with white, pink, or purple flowers. Blazing star is of the *Liatris* genus, which are known as meadow or prairie flowers.

AVAILABILITY
Summer to early fall

CONDITIONING TIPS
Blazing stars are best harvested when the top flowers have opened but before the bottom flowers have opened. The stalks will continue to open fully over a period of a couple weeks. As the old flowers at the top begin to look spent, snip them off, and the stalk will continue putting out fresh blooms down the stem. Blazing stars provide great textural and vertical interest to casual vase arrangements and are often used in summer wedding bouquets.

FASCINATING FACTS
Native Americans ground the roots of the blazing star to treat fevers and as a pain reliever for headaches, arthritis, and earaches. The leaves were used as a treatment for an upset stomach and as an antiseptic wash.

Dianthus, Green Trick

(Green Ball, Globe Carnation)

With its round, furry green blooms, green trick is a special dianthus breed that actually does not flower. The "flower" is actually made up of soft filaments sitting atop a sturdy carnation-like stem. It looks very much like sweet William, but it is not. Let's call it a close cousin.

AVAILABILITY
All year

CONDITIONING TIPS
Like other carnations, the green trick will remain fresh and healthy looking for 14 days, as long as you remove the foliage and change the water regularly.

FASCINATING FACTS
This mutant was originally discarded by people in breeding test fields because it had no real flower. Nature's mistake is a floral designer's good fortune.

Dianthus, Single Carnation

(Common Carnation, Flower of the Gods)

Common carnations' natural colors are pinkish purples, but now, thanks to selective breeding, they are offered in every color imaginable. These delicate single multi-petaled blossoms at the end of a long stem are popular because they have a very long vase life. They are hybridized and often dyed in a rainbow of colors, and they are generally cost effective.

AVAILABILITY
All year

CONDITIONING TIPS
Carnations are the most underrated flower. They can remain fresh for 14 days, as long as you remove the foliage and change the water every 2 or 3 days.

FASCINATING FACTS
Carnations have a very subtle and beautiful fragrance. It is balmy and spicy and evokes the aroma of cloves and grass—yet another reason to buy this underrated flower. If you're having trouble figuring out what to do with carnations, try using twenty or thirty in a vase for unexpected impact.

Dianthus,
Spray Carnation

Spray carnations are smaller versions of the common carnation and have multiple blooms per stem. It is hybridized and dyed to reveal a host of magical colors.

AVAILABILITY
All year

CONDITIONING TIPS
Like other carnations, these can remain fresh for 14 days. Just remove the foliage and change the water regularly to prevent the water from growing too much bacteria.

FASCINATING FACTS
This variety doesn't have a fragrance that can be detected easily.

Dianthus, Sweet William

Sweet William has many brightly colored miniature flowers blooming from a crown of green.

AVAILABILITY
All year

CONDITIONING TIPS
Like other carnations, these can remain fresh for 14 days. Just remove the foliage and change the water regularly.

FASCINATING FACTS
Sweet William is the flowering version of the green trick carnation—the only difference between the two is that one flowers and one does not. Ironically, the one that doesn't flower is much more popular than the one that does.

Dusty Miller
(*Jacobaea maritima*)

(Silver Dust, Silver Ragwort, Maritime Ragwort)

This fun foliage is silver-gray and fuzzy, making it great for winter arrangements, even though it actually blooms in the summer.

AVAILABILITY
All year

CONDITIONING TIPS
This foliage needs *lots* of hydration. Skin the stems and cone all the foliage while it's still wet. Once coned, place the skinned stems in extremely hot water.

FASCINATING FACTS
Dusty miller brings an elegance to any flower arrangement when green just isn't cutting it. The bright silvery foliage contrasts well with bright blossoms and particularly looks great with pinks, blushes, and whites.

Echinacea

(Coneflower)

Echinaceas are colorful, daisy-like flowers with raised cone-like centers.
Although purple is the most abundant, coneflower colors include pink, red,
orange, white, and yellow. Most are single-petaled blooms, but double and
triple blooms are also available. The thin stem is covered with coarse hairs.

AVAILABILITY
Early summer to early fall

CONDITIONING TIPS
Remove foliage and cut the stem on an angle. Hydrate in a solution of
warm water and flower food for 2 hours before arranging. Coneflower
petals dry or wilt easily, but the centers can be used for 7 to 10 days or in
dried arrangements.

FASCINATING FACTS
Purple coneflowers are the primary ingredient in herbal teas designed to
strengthen the immune system. Pioneers nicknamed the plant the thirst
plant because eating the purple coneflower's roots helped reduce a person's
thirst when water was scarce.

Eremurus

(Foxtail Lily, Desert Candle)

Eremurus is known for its impressive bottle-brush flowers, which can rise to a height of more than 7 feet. The blossoms are available in white, pink, yellow, and orange.

AVAILABILITY
Late spring to early summer

CONDITIONING TIPS
Cut and put in treated room temperature water. Expected vase life averages about 10 days. Because eremurus lasts for such a long time, the water should be changed often.

FASCINATING FACTS
This plant is actually made up of thousands of flowers that bloom from the bottom up. The giant bloom spikes are terrific for making a statement in larger arrangements and at events.

Eryngium

(Sea Holly, Blue Thistle)

This flowering herb is treasured for its exquisite color and unique shape. The basal leaves in shades of silver, green, blue, or purple are topped with thistle-like flower heads encased by spiny bracts (modified leaves). Each flower is a composite of tiny violet-blue florets.

AVAILABILITY
All year

CONDITIONING TIPS
Cut the stems at a 45-degree angle and strip any foliage that falls below the waterline. Hydrate them in room temperature water. Refrigerating the stems for up to 2 days intensifies the color. Eryngium is also suitable for drying with a silica gel.

FASCINATING FACTS
Eryngium is a versatile filler flower, complementing almost all color palettes and adding great visual interest. In herbal medicine, eryngium root has been used to treat coughs and liver diseases and in tonics as a diuretic and stimulant.

Eucalyptus

Many types of eucalyptus are used in floral design, but the most popular are seeded eucalyptus, baby blue and silver dollar, pictured here. Eucalyptus foliage is a great filler that smells delicious and has a wonderful silver-blue to gray-green color.

AVAILABILITY
All year

CONDITIONING TIPS
Eucalyptus is an oily plant and does not absorb water like other materials. However, giving the stems a fresh cut, putting them into super hot water, and misting this foliage will help keep them looking fresh.

FASCINATING FACTS
Eucalyptus trees can range from 33 feet to more than 200 feet in height. Aboriginal Australians use the plant as a remedy for fevers, wounds, joint pain, coughs, and even asthma. The fragrant oil from the leaves has antiseptic, anti-inflammatory, and antibacterial properties.

Fern

Ferns come in a variety of unique shades, leaf shapes, and thicknesses. The sword fern, a tropical fern that has a sharp triangular shape and a cheery green color, is an excellent choice for use with arrangements because it is hardy and won't lose its color.

AVAILABILITY
All year

CONDITIONING TIPS
Strip any leaves that will be under water level. Ferns are a great neutral backdrop to an arrangement. Use them to help space out big or highly colorful blooms, give contrast between elements, and help bulk up areas with smaller flowers. They can last 7 to 10 days.

FASCINATING FACTS
Ferns can enhance a traditional arrangement by giving it a wildflower feeling. Since ferns are often seen growing wild in the woodland, they can bring a natural feel to bouquets.

Forsythia

(Golden Bells)

Forsythia is one of the first signs of spring; its bright yellow bell-shaped flowers burst forth before its leaves. The foliage is attractive, but the shrub's real attraction is when its branches glow yellow.

AVAILABILITY

Spring

CONDITIONING TIPS

Forsythias make great, showy cut flowers. You don't have to wait until spring to get blooms. You can force the branches by simply cutting a few stems and placing them in warm water. In about 7 days, blooms should appear. They can last up to 21 days with consistent fresh water.

FASCINATING FACTS

Forsythia belongs to the same family as the olive. The yellow flowers are edible and can add cheery color to salads or garnishes. They can be used to make syrup or tea.

Freesia

Freesia flowers are known for their delicate appearance, bright colors, and wonderful aroma. The bell-shaped freesia blossoms bloom in a similar way to gladiola, in that the flowers grow from a central stalk that has sword-shaped leaves. They come in a wide range of colors, including white, pink, yellow, and a beautiful blush. Stems are typically around 12 inches in height.

AVAILABILITY
All year

CONDITIONING TIPS
Look for freesia with straight stems and at least seven buds, with only the first few open. Gently remove all non-blooming florets and leaves to reveal the individual stems. The unopened buds are fragile, so you must be careful. Cut the stem on an angle and place in a vase of warm water. The florets you have removed will not open, but they can be a nice addition to any arrangement.

FASCINATING FACTS
Freesia plants are zygomorphic, which means that the flowers only grow on one side of the stalk. Freesia has a wonderful fresh fragrance that is reminiscent of sweet cut grass. If you want highly scented freesia, look for the pink and red varieties.

Fritillaria

(Checkered Lily, Fox's Grape)

Fritillaria comes in sizes ranging from big to small and in some impressive colors: red, orange, yellow, and purple as well as white with a checkered pattern. There are also some curious variants of green with brown and orange spots, green with purple stripes, and burgundy with yellow edges.

AVAILABILITY
Winter to early summer

CONDITIONING TIPS
With their eye-catching delicate and delightful bell shapes, fritillaria can create a gorgeous moody bouquet, particularly in an interesting vase with other spring bloomers, because they all like to show off. Put in cold water because it's an early spring flower with a soft stem.

FASCINATING FACTS
The fragrance of the flower smells a lot like marijuana, so florists sometimes refer to it as the marijuana flower. Fritillaria has been making waves with floral designers recently and can be pricey.

Fritillaria, Crown Imperial

Fritillaria imperialis bears a beautiful display of drooping flowers at the top of the stem, topped by a crown of small leaves, hence the name. Along the stem are glossy lance-shaped leaves. Crown varieties include persica, imperialis maxima, persica green dreams, and crown imperial yellow. It comes in shades of red, orange, and yellow.

AVAILABILITY
Spring

CONDITIONING TIPS
These tall fritillaria varieties have many delicate leaves on the stems, which are generally left on unless they are damaged in transit. If they are damaged, they should be removed. The water temperature should be cold, due to fritillaria's soft stems.

FASCINATING FACTS
Gardeners love the crown imperial not just for its tall, striking beauty, but because the bulbs have a pungent smell that is known to keep rodents at bay.

Ginger
(*Etlingera elatior*)

(Torch Ginger, Ginger Lily)

Ginger is known for its ostrich-like plumes, which are actually not blooms but bright red or pink bracts (modified leaves). The actual flower of the ginger plant is tiny and white.

AVAILABILITY
All year

CONDITIONING TIPS
Ginger is often an attention-getter in an arrangement and will last in a vase from 7 to 14 days. To keep ginger going, change the water every 2 days and bathe the entire ginger bloom in room temperature water for up to 10 minutes. After the soak, cut off a ½ inch of the stem before replacing it in the vase.

FASCINATING FACTS
Ginger's elegant bloom clusters, enthralling scent, and variety of shapes and sizes make it a great statement flower in arrangements. Ginger flowers are grown separately from ginger that is edible.

Gladiolus

(Sword Lily)

The gladiolus has an array of beautiful, brightly colored trumpet-shaped blooms on a tall stalk. Florists love using gladiolus spikes to add a striking pop of color and vertical accent to arrangements.

AVAILABILITY
Summer

CONDITIONING TIPS
Look for stems that have a few buds at least a quarter open. Cut the stalks on the diagonal and place in a container filled with warm water. Letting the container sit in a cool, dark place before arranging will extend their vase life. Trim 1 inch of each stalk every few days, and snip off lower flowers as they fade.

FASCINATING FACTS
The botanical name *Gladiolus* is a nod to Roman gladiators, who fought with swords. The flower symbolizes love at first sight and looks spectacular in bouquets and vases.

Gloriosa Lily (*Gloriosa* spp.)

(Fire Lily, Flame Lily, Creeping Lily, Cat's Claw)

Not a true lily, but a member of the autumn crocus family, the gloriosa lily's pink and yellow flower has six distinct petals that make the flower look almost inside out, like an umbrella caught in a sudden gust. The petals and six stamens turn deep rose as it ages. Other varieties are available as well, including dwarf, yellow, orange-yellow, and deep red.

AVAILABILITY
Late spring to fall

CONDITIONING TIPS
Eye-catching gloriosa is an excellent, long-lasting cut flower. It adds great sculptural interest to an arrangement but is bold enough to stand alone. Be aware that the bright orange pollen of the gloriosa will leave an indelible stain. For this reason, some floral designers remove the pollen-bearing anthers at the end of the stamens.

FASCINATING FACTS
All parts of the gloriosa are poisonous, especially the seeds and tubers, so take special care when working with them and make sure pets and children don't chew on them. Despite its beauty, gloriosa in the wild is often considered an invasive weed.

Gomphrena

(Globe Amaranth)

These globe-shaped, clover-like blossoms in shades of purple, red, pink, yellow, and white sit atop upright spikes. These "flowers" are actually papery bracts (or modified leaves). The real flowers grow within these bracts and are barely visible.

AVAILABILITY
Summer through first frost

CONDITIONING TIPS
Give the stems a fresh diagonal cut, remove as much foliage as possible, and put them in hot water with plenty of antibacterials. This will keep the flowers from becoming moldy, which is an issue because they last so long.

FASCINATING FACTS
Gomphrena make good dried flowers because they retain their color and shape. When the blooms are completely open, but not too old, simply cut and hang them upside down in bunches to dry. They can be used on the stems, or the globes can be removed for other projects. As a dried flower, they might just last forever.

Gypsophila

(Baby's Breath, Soap Root, Chalk Plant)

Baby's breath has delicate stems with graceful consistent-sized or variable-sized flowers with five petals. It is typically white with tints of either pink or lavender.

AVAILABILITY
All year; naturally blooms in late spring

CONDITIONING TIPS
Baby's breath is the Velcro of the flower industry. It can be used alone, mono-floral, or in small clusters, and it is great mixed with other summer field flowers. The trick when working with it is to separate it into usable bits and not use it in matted clumps. When baby's breath is shipped, it needs to be uncoupled by moving one stem either up or down while pulling them gently apart.

FASCINATING FACTS
The baby's breath flower has saponins, chemicals that have the ability to break down some cancer cells.

Hedera

(Ivy)

Hedera foliage is green or variegated. When it goes to seed, its black seeds make for striking designs.

AVAILABILITY
All year

CONDITIONING TIPS
Bush ivy's long stems and branching leaves keep well and retain their fresh appearance for a while. Cut the stems with a sharp knife, lay the woody ends on a countertop, and hammer the bottoms of the stems gently. Crushing the stems allows for more water absorption.

FASCINATING FACTS
Bush ivy stems and leaves are easy to work with for garlands and tabletop decor, and they can even be used as garnish on hors d'oeuvres trays. It is most commonly harvested from buildings or cemeteries, but it also grows in the wild.

Heliconia

(Lobster Claw, Wild Plantain, Bird of Paradise)

Heliconia is found in rainforests and the wet tropics. Their brightly colored flowers, typically red, yellow, and orange, are actually waxy bracts. Some heliconia plants have upright bracts, while others dangle; the latter are referred to as hanging heliconia.

AVAILABILITY
All year

CONDITIONING TIPS
Heliconias are a striking addition to arrangements, adding height and a fresh tropical vibe. Avoid picking stems that are dried or have black spots. Before designing, use a sharp knife to cut 3 inches of the stem underwater. To give them some extra support, use wire and floral foam. With fresh water, vase life can be anywhere from 7 to 21 days.

FASCINATING FACTS
Heliconia's colorful bracts are so large they almost completely hide its flowers. This keeps the flower's delicious nectar reserved for specialized creatures like hummingbirds and butterflies.

Helleborus

(Hellebore, Lenten Rose)

There are nearly two dozen species and many hybrids of hellebores that come in a beautiful array of earthy shades, including pink, mauve, green, buttery yellow, creamy white, and a near-black burgundy. There are varieties with double blooms and some that are even striped and daintily speckled.

AVAILABILITY
Spring

CONDITIONING TIPS
Hellebores last longest when they are cut after the flower heads have dropped their stamens and the central seed pods have formed. This is when the stems are visibly rigid, so the flower is strong and sturdy. It is best to wait until they are fully grown before using them. If you are in a position where your flowers are still young and the stamens are still attached, submerge the flower entirely in cold, clean water for 12 to 24 hours to help hydrate it.

FASCINATING FACTS
Hellebores' delicately cupped, nodding heads and big, jagged edged leaves are sometimes tricky to work with in compositions, but they can add a touch of self-assured elegance to simpler designs. The natural droop of their flowers can spill over the edge of small vases to create a graceful design, or they can always confidently stand alone in a bud vase.

Holly (*Ilex* spp.)

Holly is known for its dark green spiny leaves and bright red berries. Holly's glossy leaves look good all year long. The leaves of many species have wavy margins tipped with spines. Holly is dioecious, meaning that each holly plant is either male or female. Bushes with berries are always female, while those without might be male or female.

AVAILABILITY
All year; berries in the fall and winter

CONDITIONING TIPS
When you get fresh cut holly, wash it. Giving holly a good rinse removes any contaminants, such as dust and garden residue. Place branches in hot water. Holly will stay fresh in water for 7 to 21 days.

FASCINATING FACTS
Thanks to its evergreen nature, holly has long been thought to deter evil spirits and witches. This is why in the depth of winter, when everything else appeared dead and lifeless, sprigs of vibrant green holly loaded with berries were brought inside and hung around the house to ward away evil.

Horsetail Fern (*Equisetum* spp.)

(Snake Grass)

Horsetail ferns, with their hollow fluted stems and feathery branches, look more like grasses or reeds than they do ferns. The 10- to 24-inch-tall stem has pronounced rings, similar to bamboo, and light green feather-like leaves grow horizontally from the rings, creating a cylindrical form.

AVAILABILITY
All year

CONDITIONING TIPS
Horsetail ferns are perfect for contemporary arrangements' linear design. Their hollow stem is very malleable and can be bent to form geometric shapes. Wire can also be run through the hollow stem to help keep it in a desired shape.

FASCINATING FACTS
Horsetail fern is a living fossil, the last remaining genus in the class Equisetopsida. They have been basically the same since the Paleozoic era.

Hosta

(Plantain Lily)

Hostas are known for their attractive showy foliage with leaves that are wonderful for their diversity of size, color, and texture. Hostas come in a variety of colors, including green, blue-green, yellow, variegated, and even white, and the leaves come in a variety of shapes and sizes, ranging from heart shaped to sword shaped. Hostas also produces spikes of lily-like flowers in white or lavender.

AVAILABILITY
Summer

CONDITIONING TIPS
Hosta leaves are popular vase fillers, giving flower arrangements extra dimension. They are versatile and easy to work with. After cutting the stems, plunge them into ice cold water. Change the water every few days, and hosta leaves will look great for a couple weeks.

FASCINATING FACTS
Hosta buds and blossoms are edible. The buds look similar to baby artichokes and are delicious fried or steamed and dipped in butter. The blossoms are sweet and can be added to salads or even sugared for use as decorative flourishes on desserts.

Hyacinth (*Hyacinthus* spp.)

(Muscari)

Hyacinth's sweet perfume and gorgeous, tightly packed bell-shaped florets are a welcome sign of early spring, whether sticking out of the ground or in buckets at the flower shop. They come in a range of colors, including white, cream, yellow, pink, a variety of blues, purple, lilac, and even multicolored.

AVAILABILITY
Spring

CONDITIONING TIPS
To make hyacinths grow to their fullest potential, drop the entire stem, leaves, and bulb (if present) into ice cold water, which should be replaced every other day to keep them fresh. Hyacinth flowers can become top-heavy, so a bamboo cocktail stick delicately inserted into the stem can offer needed support. Hyacinths will last in a vase roughly 7 to 10 days if they are well tended.

FASCINATING FACTS
With their rich colors and scents, hyacinths are a great flower for spring wedding bouquets and work well when mixed with other seasonal flowers like hydrangeas and stocks. The story of how hyacinths came to be known around the world: a ship from the east carrying these bulbs sank off the coast of Holland, and the following year thousands of hyacinths sprouted on the banks of the North Sea, making them the "it" flower of 1734. They are now mainly sourced from Holland.

Hydrangea, Lacecap

Lacecap hydrangeas belong to the bigleaf hydrangea species, which are native to Japan. Their flower heads are surrounded by showier, sporadically raised flowers that look like flat caps with frilly edges, which give them the lacy quality for which they're known.

AVAILABILITY
May through November; peak: July through September

CONDITIONING TIPS
Hydrangeas are thirsty flowers and should be put in hot water right away, and the water should be changed every couple of days. The big secret to keeping hydrangeas looking fresh is cutting and splitting the stems (or smashing them with a hammer) and scraping off the outer shell with a knife or other blade. Then spray the colorful pom-poms with water a few times every day. Vase life will be about 10 days. If you want your hydrangeas to last longer, dry them. To do this, place them in a vase with just a few inches of water and leave them. As the water evaporates, the hydrangeas will dry; once dried, they can last for a year or more.

FASCINATING FACTS
Lacecap hydrangeas can grow up to 7 feet tall.

Hydrangea, Oakleaf

Oakleaf hydrangeas have a pyramidal cluster of white blooms and leaves that look like those of an oak tree, but even bigger. The blooms turn purple as they age in a process known as antiquing.

AVAILABILITY
May through November; peak: July through September

CONDITIONING TIPS
Hydrangeas are thirsty flowers and should be put in hot water right away, and the water should be changed every couple of days. The big secret to keeping hydrangeas looking fresh is cutting and splitting the stems (or smashing them with a hammer) and scraping off the outer shell with a knife or other blade. Then spray the colorful pom-poms with water a few times every day. Vase life will be about 10 days. If you want your hydrangeas to last longer, dry them. To do this, place them in a vase with just a few inches of water and leave them. As the water evaporates, the hydrangeas will dry; once dried, they can last for a year or more.

FASCINATING FACTS
Oakleaf hydrangeas are commonly grown in the southeastern United States, from North Carolina to Florida, and as far west as Louisiana.

Hydrangea, Peegee

Peegee hydrangeas produce showy, snowball white blooms in a stunning spray that fade to pink, bronze, and brown as they age. The dark green, oval leaves of the peegee are also attractive, and they turn bronze in the fall months.

AVAILABILITY
May through November; peak: July through September

CONDITIONING TIPS
Hydrangeas are thirsty flowers and should be put in hot water right away, and the water should be changed every couple of days. The big secret to keeping hydrangeas looking fresh is cutting and splitting the stems (or smashing them with a hammer) and scraping off the outer shell with a knife or other blade. Then spray the colorful pom-poms with water a few times every day. Vase life will be about 10 days. If you want your hydrangeas to last longer, dry them. To do this, place them in a vase with just a few inches of water and leave them. As the water evaporates, the hydrangeas will dry; once dried, they can last for a year or more.

FASCINATING FACTS
There are over seventy-five species and varieties of hydrangeas, and they come in various shapes, sizes, and colors, including blue, pink, red, purple, green, and white.

Hydrangea, Standard

There are more than seventy-five species of hydrangeas, six of the major ones being bigleaf, smooth, panicle, oakleaf, climbing, and mountain. Their unmistakable pom-pom clusters of florets with starlike petals have colors determined by the pH level in the soil. The beautiful petals—in purple, pink, white, or blue—are actually sepals, leaves that protect the flower bud.

AVAILABILITY
May through November; peak: July through September

CONDITIONING TIPS
Hydrangeas are thirsty flowers and should be put in hot water right away, and the water should be changed every couple days. The big secret to keeping hydrangeas looking fresh is cutting and splitting the stems (or smashing them with a hammer) and scraping off the outer shell with a knife or blade. Then spray the colorful pom-poms with water a few times every day. Vase life will be about 10 days. If you want your hydrangeas to last longer, dry them. To do this, place them in a vase with just a few inches of water and leave them. As the water evaporates, the hydrangeas will dry; once dried, they can last for a year or more.

FASCINATING FACTS
Hydrangeas contain low levels of cyanide. Although it's a small amount of poison, it's enough to be a danger to both humans and pets if ingested.

Hypericum

(St. John's Wort)

Hypericum has leafy stems that are 24 to 36 inches long with clusters of round berries at the top. There are more than four hundred cultivars of hypericum, one-third of which are used as ornamental cut flowers. They come in a wide range of colors, such as red, brown, ivory, pink, and burgundy, but the most common are tiny yellow star-shaped flowers and lush, dark green foliage.

AVAILABILITY
All year; especially popular during winter

CONDITIONING TIPS
The flowers are pretty, but the clusters of ornamental berries are great filler to add a burst of color and texture to bouquets, arrangements, and centerpieces. Put them in hot water, and they will last 5 to 7 days.

FASCINATING FACTS
The nickname St. John's wort is derived from the feast honoring St. John the Baptist, in which tradition is to pluck the herb on the night of the feast and take it to church to be blessed, as the herb was believed to have special powers to ward off evil spirits. Hippocrates, the father of medicine, almost 2,400 years ago, recommended St. John's wort to treat nervous unrest. Its hypericin is believed to produce sedative and pain-relieving effects.

Iris, Bearded

The bearded iris flower has three upright petals, called standards, and three cascading petals, called falls. Additionally, there is usually an entire second flower behind the first one, which yields a second bloom. The hybrid varieties come in some of the most stunning colors and shades imaginable. There is never just one shade.

AVAILABILITY

Early summer

CONDITIONING TIPS

The best irises come in early summer from the Pacific Northwest. Most people don't realize that each bloom has a second bloom right behind the first. When the first bloom looks wilty, snap it off and let the second one dazzle you. There are usually several blooms per stem, up to six or more.

FASCINATING FACTS

In Greek mythology, Iris was the personification of the rainbow and a messenger from the gods. An extract from the iris, called orris root, is used as an additive for perfumes and potpourri. Orris is also an ingredient in some brands of gin.

Iris, Standard

Irises come in many forms, shapes, and sizes and can be found in every color of the rainbow, but most common are purple, blue, white, and yellow. Flowers consist of three upward oriented petals, called standards, and three downward oriented sepals, known as falls. The long, swordlike stems may be simple or branched and range in height from 8 inches to 3 feet.

AVAILABILITY
Early summer

CONDITIONING TIPS
Remove the foliage from the base of the stem and split the two leaves covering the flower at the top. (If not removed, the flower will have trouble blooming.) Then place these soft stemmed beauties in cold water.

FASCINATING FACTS
The fleur-de-lis is a graphic representation of the iris.

Kalanchoe

(Christmas Kalanchoe, Flaming Katy)

Kalanchoe is a succulent with stems that have large, dark green leaves with scalloped edges and tubular-shaped flowers featuring four petals (or up to twenty-six petals in double flowering varieties). It comes in a variety of colors, including red, pink, orange, white, yellow, lilac, coral, salmon, and bicolor.

AVAILABILITY
All year

CONDITIONING TIPS
With a stem length of around 2 feet, kalanchoe is a great filler flower. Put it in room temperature water and change often. Kalanchoe can last from 14 to 21 days in a vase. It can add a happy pop of color for bridal bouquets and centerpieces.

FASCINATING FACTS
In 1971, kalanchoe seeds were sent up to space to cheer up the lonely and depressed Soviet Salyut 1 space station crew. The little seedlings were named "life tree" and were featured in television broadcasts from the space station. One warning: despite the nickname, its blossoms contain cardiac glycosides that are toxic to animals, so keep this pretty blossom away from pets!

Kale (*Brassica oleracea*)

Kale "flowers" are actually lush heads of ruffled leaves. They come in cream, green, pink, purple, red, and white.

AVAILABILITY
All year

CONDITIONING TIPS
Ornamental kale offers unique colors and can give a spectacular texture to arrangements. Peel the outer layer of leaves one at a time to form a rosette. Cut the stems at an angle with a sharp knife.

FASCINATING FACTS
Ornamental kales and their cousins, ornamental cabbages, were developed for their colors, not their taste. Because they are bitter, they don't make good food, but their unique symmetry, interesting texture, and vibrant color do make beautiful additions to arrangements and create a nice garnish on hors d'oeuvres plates.

Kangaroo Paw (*Anigozanthos* spp.)

With its cheerful clusters of velvety tubular flowers coated with dense hairs and six clawlike structures, the kangaroo paw definitely resembles marsupial toes. Its tall stems of blossoms come in a rainbow of colors, including orange, red, burgundy, yellow, pink, and bicolored.

AVAILABILITY
All year

CONDITIONING TIPS
When selecting kangaroo paws, look for buds that are plump, not shriveled, and the flowers shouldn't be droopy. Cutting underwater will help reduce the risk of air pockets forming, and because these are desert flowers, they need to be placed in very hot water. Kangaroo paws are thirsty, so keeping them recut and well watered will help them last from 6 to 14 days.

FASCINATING FACTS
Native to Western Australia, the kangaroo paw adds a little whimsy to contemporary design. The extract of kangaroo paw flowers is used in skincare products to encourage cell growth and keep skin looking youthful and wrinkle free.

Larkspur

(Rocket Larkspur, Lark's Claw, Lark's Heel)

With its tall, airy stalks of colorful blossoms and lacy, dark green foliage, larkspur has become a floral favorite. It's a member of the *Delphinium* genus, and its flower spikes come in shades of sky blue to deep blue, pink, and white.

AVAILABILITY
All year

CONDITIONING TIPS
The hollow larkspur stems can break, so support them if needed. Remove as much foliage and florets from the stems as possible, give the stems a fresh cut with a florist's knife, and place in warm water with plenty of antibacterials. Vase life is 5 to 7 days.

FASCINATING FACTS
The alluring flower shape and colors of larkspurs make them charming cut flowers and stunning additions to any bouquet. In ancient times, the seeds of larkspurs were used to get rid of lice, and in Transylvania, larkspurs were planted around stables to keep witches from casting spells on the animals.

Lavender
(*Lavandula* spp.)

Considering this plant has the same name as a color, you might think that its graceful spikes might all be shades of purple, but the more than forty-five species of lavender and more than 450 varieties come in different colors, including white, pink, and yellow.

AVAILABILITY

All year

CONDITIONING TIPS

Before putting lavender in water, remove any of the silver-green foliage that will be below water level and give the stems a clean cut. Changing the water daily and keeping them out of direct sunlight will help them last longer. If you want a long-lasting lavender, dry it. Simply gather a bunch, secure the stems with twine, and hang the bouquet anywhere it will stay dry. Your bouquet will last (and hold its scent!) for 2 years. If the scent fades, bring it into a steamy bathroom or spritz it with warm water.

FASCINATING FACTS

During the Black Plague in the 14th century, lavender oil was used to fend off the disease, and bunches of it were sold in the streets to mask the smell of the dead. Queen Victoria, ruler of Great Britain in the 19th century, was such a fan of lavender that she sipped lavender tea and had all her furniture polished with a lavender-infused solution. Want to like it even more? The fragrance of lavender is known to repel bugs.

Leucadendron

Leucadendrons are simple yet fiery shrubs with very solid-looking hardy "flowers," which consist of a cone-like flower head enclosed by colored leaflike bracts at the top of the stem. They come in single stems or in sprays and a variety of colors: red, green, yellow, orange, burgundy, and silver.

AVAILABILITY
All year

CONDITIONING TIPS
This is a hardy variety, which needs only a fresh cut and room temperature or hot water. Remove as little foliage as possible.

FASCINATING FACTS
Leucadendron plants' foliage offers color, texture, and a long vase life for big floral display and combines well with succulents, pine, and ornamental grasses.

Lilac (*Syringa* spp.)

There are several different variations of flowering lilac. The colors range from white to light blue to purple to blush pink. They are grown in single or double petal varieties. It takes 2 years for each plant to produce a flower worthy of exporting.

AVAILABILITY
Early spring

CONDITIONING TIPS
Lilacs are known to love moisture, but only on the stems and not on the flower, or it will wilt. Smash the bottom 2 inches of the stem, scrape the excess off, spray the stems for added moisture, and place them in a vase of hot water and flower food.

FASCINATING FACTS
Known as the Queen of Shrubs, lilacs are in the same family as olives. Lilacs were grown in some of early America's first botanical gardens, and both George Washington and Thomas Jefferson grew them.

Lily, Hybrid (*Lilium* spp.)

(Stargazer, Casa Blanca, Martagon)

Lilies are known for large, robust, upright blooms and strong, enchanting scents. Lilies are diverse and colorful and have dramatic blooms. It's no wonder they are some of the most popular flowers in the world.

AVAILABILITY
Summer

CONDITIONING TIPS
Removing the stamen and placing the flower immediately in water will help your lilies open brighter and faster. Lilies are a long-lasting cut bloom with a good vase life.

FASCINATING FACTS
Lilies are poisonous to cats, so keep your furry felines away from them.

Lily, Nerine (*Nerine* spp.)

(Spider Lily, Guernsey Lily, Cape Flower)

The nerine lily has between six and ten individual flowers that resemble a hybrid lily, with curved flower petals and stamens, but it also has much skinnier and longer flower petals. It is called a spider lily because when fully bloomed, it looks like an arachnid. Nerines are available in a wide range of pinks, from pale blush to hot pink, and also in deep red, reddish orange, and pure white.

AVAILABILITY
Summer through early fall

CONDITIONING TIPS
Look for straight stems with opening flowers, as tightly closed buds tend not to open. The nerine lily does not come with leaves. After giving it a fresh cut and placing it in clean water, remove the collar around the neck of the flower, because it becomes brown after 1 or 2 days. These lilies are sensitive to ethylene gas, so keep them away from fruit. Vase life is 7 to 14 days.

FASCINATING FACTS
The nerine lily got its nickname Guernsey lily when a ship wrecked many years ago on Guernsey, an island off the coast of Normandy. They are native only to South Africa and bloom every March atop Table Mountain in Cape Town.

Lily of the Valley (*Convallaria majalis*)

(May Flower, May Bell)

These nodding bell-shaped flowers are in a cluster on one side of a leafless stalk and are traditionally white but sometimes lavender. The two glossy leaves rise up from the base of the plant.

AVAILABILITY
Spring

CONDITIONING TIPS
These lovely flowers are very delicate. Most florists keep the leaves on the stems as long as possible to protect the flowers. Give them a fresh cut with a knife and put in clean, cold water.

FASCINATING FACTS
The sweet-smelling white flowers of lily of the valley have long been associated with the feminine virtues of chastity, pureness, and sweetness. They are a wedding favorite. Queen Victoria, Grace Kelly, and Kate Middleton all used the dainty, bell-shaped buds in their wedding bouquets.

Limonium

(Statice, Sea Lavender, Marsh Rosemary)

Limonium has branched, hairy stems topped with clusters of petite, papery florets. Its blossoms feature white corollas and calyxes, and they are available in white, pink, yellow, lavender, and purple, the most popular. Its stems range from around 12 to 18 inches in height.

AVAILABILITY
All year

CONDITIONING TIPS
Limonium has great texture and is a popular filler flower, working well in both fresh and dried arrangements. Known as the everlasting flower, limonium blooms boast a super long vase life and retain most of their color even when dried. Even though limonium is beautiful, some people say the blossoms have a pungent scent. The smell is lessened if it's kept in cool, well-ventilated spots.

FASCINATING FACTS
Limonium has been used in herbal remedies to treat a variety of problems, including diarrhea, dysentery, and laryngitis.

Lisianthus
(*Eustoma* spp.)

(Prairie Gentian)

With its ruffly blossoms, lisianthus is a stunning flower often mistaken for a rose or peony. Each blossom spirals open in a loose, five-petaled papery funnel. Colors include purple, lilac, peach, red, yellow, white, and bicolored. There are mini as well as extra-double varieties, and new hybrids are introduced every year.

AVAILABILITY
All year

CONDITIONING TIPS
Select stems with two or three open flowers and the rest of the buds closed but beginning to show traces of color. Flowers that are too open will bruise in transit, and buds that are too tightly closed will wither without opening. Handle with care, as the petals are very soft and delicate. Note that they don't like humidity. Cut the stems, remove all of the foliage, and place in hot treated water.

FASCINATING FACTS
Lisianthus is native to North America, where it is known as prairie gentian. It grows in riverbeds and on prairies in Texas, Nebraska, Nevada, and Colorado. In the 1930s, Japanese flower breeders took wild prairie gentian and created the beloved modern lisianthus.

Lysimachia

(Loosestrife, Gooseneck Loosestrife, Moneywort,
Purple Willow Herb)

Lysimachia looks a lot like veronica (page 330), but it is not. It has larger
leaves and a spike-shaped arching flower head. Varieties include white,
yellow, and crimson flowers.

AVAILABILITY
Summer

CONDITIONING TIPS
Select straight, sturdy stems with about one-half of their florets open.
Remove all the foliage, as it wilts and kills the flower quickly. Cut and
place in warm to hot water.

FASCINATING FACTS
According to a 3,000-year-old Macedonian legend, King Lysimachus of
Thrace used this flower to calm a mad ox. Its common name loosestrife is
derived from the Greek word that means to "end strife."

Matricaria

(Chamomile, Mayweed)

Chamomile flowers' delicate apple-scented blooms consist of yellow disc-shaped florets and white ray-shaped florets. Matricaria has many relatives in the plant world; however, only two common ones are used in the cut flower world: chamomile and feverfew. They are almost indistinguishable, except that chamomile has a rounded bottom.

AVAILABILITY
Summer to fall

CONDITIONING TIPS
Like all others, it is important to remove as much of the foliage as possible. It is also helpful to separate the flowers from each other as they tend to get tangled. It's best to edit each stem down so there aren't too many flowers on each stem.

FASCINATING FACTS
Chamomile is most well known for its medicinal traits. It has a strong apple-like fragrance and is the main ingredient to most sleep-inducing teas.

Moluccella

(Bells of Ireland, Shell Flower)

Bells of Ireland sport green, bell-shaped calyxes on tall, stringy stems. They are also sometimes tinted red. They can reach up to 3 feet in height.

AVAILABILITY
All year

CONDITIONING TIPS
These flowers are fabulous shape-shifters. They can grow an additional 6 inches and become like a snake. They like a fresh cut with a knife. Remove the bells below the waterline. Designers beware: bells have a forked thorn at the base of each flower, which looks harmless but can penetrate deep into your skin if you're not careful.

FASCINATING FACTS
When using these plants in your garden, it is best to plant them behind your tulips, because they have a similar line shape and are a good complement. The same is true when making a flower arrangement with bells: mix them with other line flowers. The flower continues to grow and has wonderful leaves that come out from the tip. Their Celtic name comes thanks to their bell-like shape and sprightly green color; they are a symbol of luck—the luck of the Irish.

Monkshood (*Aconitum* spp.)

(Wolfsbane, Blue Rocket, Friar's Cap)

Monkshood has beautiful clusters of hooded flowers that come in shades of blue. The leaves are glossy, dark green, and lobed. While blue is the classic color, there are cultivars with blooms in yellow, pink, white, and bicolored.

AVAILABILITY
All year

CONDITIONING TIPS
Monkshood, with its brilliant blue blossoms, adds color, height, and beauty to any arrangement—but note that it is one of the most deadly plants in existence. It contains aconite, a poison that can be absorbed through the skin, so it's best to use gloves when handling it, especially if you have any cuts or scrapes.

FASCINATING FACTS
Monkshood was one of the first perennials to be grown as an ornamental plant. During medieval times, juice from its roots was used to poison arrow tips for warfare and hunting.

Muscari

(Grape Hyacinth)

Muscari's tiny tubular flowers are densely clustered in spikes at stem ends, which look like upturned bunches of grapes. Muscari colors most commonly range from pale blue to navy blue, but there's also white, and its foliage resembles long blades of grass. Growing to only 6 to 8 inches in height, muscari do indeed look like miniature hyacinths.

AVAILABILITY
Early spring

CONDITIONING TIPS
Muscari's diminutive size and tightly clustered flowers make it a lovely addition to arrangements. It can last up to 6 days in vases and can also be used in dried floral arrangements. If possible, keep it with the bulb, and give it cold water as much as possible.

FASCINATING FACTS
Despite being commonly called grape hyacinth, muscaris are not hyacinths. They are members of the lily family.

Narcissus, Daffodil

(Lent Lily)

There are more than thirteen thousand daffodil varieties in existence, which can be divided into about a dozen different types characterized by the size and shape of their petals and their corona (the colorful inner petal that is often fused into a single tube).

AVAILABILITY
Spring

CONDITIONING TIPS
Daffodils don't play well with others because of the toxic calcium oxalate crystals found in the sap of cut stems. If you want to dare to mix daffodils in a vase with other flowers, first soak them in water for 24 hours. This eliminates the sap they contain, which is often poisonous to other plants. Don't cut the stems afterward, as this will trigger another release of the toxic sap. If you'd like to pair daffodils with something, try small-leaved evergreen shrubs, like boxwood or holly, because they are a bit hardier and can tolerate the daffodil's evil secretions.

FASCINATING FACTS
In ancient Rome, daffodils were prized for their sap, which was thought to contain healing properties. Daffodil bulbs contain a compound called narciclasine, which scientists have discovered may actually be effective in treating brain cancer—obviously, don't try this at home.

Narcissus, Paperwhite

(Bunchflower Daffodil)

Paperwhite refers to the star-shaped narcissus flower, which is a white spray daffodil. Flowers are white, about the size of a nickel, and come in clusters of up to a dozen blossoms per stem. Paperwhites have a distinctive sweet smell, the most fragrant of the daffodil family. This is a bulb flower that is commonly forced for the holiday season, and kits are available.

AVAILABILITY
Late fall (bulbs); early spring (cut flowers)

CONDITIONING TIPS
Paperwhites, like daffodils, secrete a poison that can harm other flowers. Therefore, it is best to give a cut and put in cold water with plenty of food to let the flower drain before adding to mixed arrangements.

FASCINATING FACTS
The custom of forcing paperwhites in a bowl of gravel filled with water is a Chinese tradition. The Chinese name for the flower is *shuixian*, which translates as "water fairy." The flowers are supposed to be the source of great happiness.

Nigella
(*Nigella damascena*)

(Love-in-a-Mist, Miss Jekyll, Love Entangle, Hair of Venus)

Nigella is an elegant and dainty ornamental flower with a beautiful star-shaped bloom, often blue, but also pink or white. Its feathery, lacelike, or filigreed leaves form a wispy, dreamlike foliage.

AVAILABILITY
August and September

CONDITIONING TIPS
Though it looks delicate, nigella isn't a particularly fussy flower. Simply cut the stems and place them in clean water. If designing for an event, work with them a couple days beforehand to give the blooms time to fully open. They have a 7- to 10-day vase life and also dry beautifully.

FASCINATING FACTS
One of nigella's many common names, love-in-a-mist, comes from its graceful fernlike foliage, which creates the appearance of mist around the flowers. Its romantic air has made nigella a popular choice among brides who hope to achieve a wildflower look.

Ninebark
(*Physocarpus* spp.)

(Diablo Ninebark)

The colorful foliage of this shrub offers four stages of maturity and many options for cutting. First, there's the flower bud stage; then, in late spring, button-like clusters of white flowers appear on its stems and are great in arrangements. They fade and leave behind small clusters of stunning seed cases that give textural accent to designs. Throughout the rest of the season, there are foliage-laden stems with serrated lobed leaves in colorful shades of deep purple, burgundy, orange, green, gold, and multihued.

AVAILABILITY
Late spring to late summer

CONDITIONING TIPS
This is a woody stem and does best when smashed with a hammer and put in a vase of hot water.

FASCINATING FACTS
How did ninebark get its name? The thin bark peels off in many layers.

Orchid
(*Cymbidium* spp.)

(Boat Orchid)

The waxy, thick flowers of cymbidium orchids have five-pointed petals on flower spikes with thin leaves. Brown, green, white, red, and yellow are the most common colors. There will be from nine to twenty blooms per stem.

AVAILABILITY
All year

CONDITIONING TIPS
Orchids are divas and need a little special care. These flowers are very heavy and will break unless given support. Most designers will attach a long bamboo stick to the stem to keep them upright. If the stem is not supported, it can break after 1 or 2 days. Depending on the type and hybrid, the blooms can last from 1 to 6 months on the plant. A cut cymbidium orchid will last up to 21 days if the water is changed every few days, the vase is kept bacteria-free, and the blooms are kept away from ripening fruits, direct sun, and heat.

FASCINATING FACTS
Cymbidium orchids go as far back as 2,500 years ago in ancient China, originating from the Himalayan Mountains and from the forests of Himalayas. Confucius, the Chinese philosopher and poet, was enamored by the exquisite beauty of orchids and dedicated many of his works to them. He dubbed the Asian cymbidium orchid as the King of Fragrance.

Orchid (*Dendrobium* spp.)

(Bamboo Orchid, Singapore Orchid)

Dendrobium is the largest genus of orchids. Dendrobiums come in varying sizes, forms, and colors. Purple and white are the two most available colors, but they also come in shades of red, pink, and yellow-green, and with curled and striped petals. Most plants produce ten to twelve flowers on each stem, with the flowers measuring 1 to 2 inches in diameter.

AVAILABILITY
All year

CONDITIONING TIPS
Refresh the blooms by completely submerging the flowers in warm water for 10 to 15 minutes or spray the flowers with a fine water mist. Then cut ¼ inch from each stem and place them in a vase of warm (100°F) water. Dendrobiums have a 7- to 14-day vase life if kept in a cool, moist environment, away from ripening fruits and dying flowers.

FASCINATING FACTS
In Greek, *dendrobium* means "life in a tree," which references that most orchids in the wild can be found attached to trees. Many dendrobium species are known to remove toxins and pollutants from the air.

Orchid (*x Mokara* spp.)

(Smile Orchid, Ladies' Finger)

The mokara orchid is a tropical flower with six to ten freckled, broad, starfish-shaped blooms per stem. The velvety blooms are 1 to 2 inches in diameter and come in a variety of colors, including red, pink, purple, orange, yellow, and gold. The elegance and graceful curves of the mokara orchid are perhaps why some refer to it as ladies' fingers, and the intricate patterns within its petals that make it look as though it's smiling are why some refer to it as the smile orchid.

AVAILABILITY
All year

CONDITIONING TIPS
Orchids often look thirsty and exhausted when they are shipped, but will quickly wake up with this routine. Remove any wrapping sleeve and completely submerge the flowers in warm (100°F) water for 10 to 15 minutes. Cut ¼ inch from the stem on an angle and put them in a vase of warm (100°F) water. To prolong their vase life, recut the stem underwater by ¼ inch every 3 days and replace the water in the vase with lukewarm water.

FASCINATING FACTS
Mokaras are a hybrid of three different types of orchids. The Indian Sanskrit word *mokara* derives from the Hindu philosophy that each individual possesses three states of well-being: the causal body, the astral body, and the physical body. *Mokara* represents the physical body.

Orchid (*Oncidium* spp.)

(Dancing Lady)

Oncidium orchids have tiny flowers that cluster in vibrant colors. Although the majority of oncidium orchids come in shades of yellow and brown, dazzling sprays in white, pink, purple, red, and green are also available. Oncidium orchids have many fluttering blooms on each stem and have been said to look like branches covered in butterflies waving in the breeze.

AVAILABILITY
All year

CONDITIONING TIPS
Cut ¼ inch from the stem and put in a clean vase of warm (100°F) water and arrange. Change the water every 3 days and add a drop of bleach to keep bacteria at bay. If using a tall variety, you might want to use a stick to help support it.

FASCINATING FACTS
Oncidium orchids were first described by Swedish botanist Olaf Swartz in 1800. The name comes from the Greek word *onkos*, which means "swelling or mass," referring to the distinctive shaped bump on the lips of its flowers.

Orchid (*Vanda* spp.)

The vanda orchid is loved for its large, fragrant, and long-lasting flowers that come in a variety of vibrant colors, including pink, yellow, red, and blue. The flower spikes generally have eight to ten blooms that rise from the base of the broad, flat leaves. Vanda orchids are monopodial plants, which means they have one stem, which grows from the top of the plant.

AVAILABILITY
All year

CONDITIONING TIPS
Vanda flowers use little water. Should the flowers begin to become somewhat limp, place the entire flower spike in water overnight. After this treatment, the flowers will refresh and be firm again. Vanda flowers are beautiful in bouquets, corsages, and flower arrangements, and a single flower can be used by placing it in a small water tube.

FASCINATING FACTS
Vandas are native to tropical climates in India and got their name from the Sanskrit word for orchid. These are "air plants" and do not need soil to grow. In the wild, they grow on trees with their roots hanging loose or wrapped around the tree. Putting a vanda in soil would cause the spongelike roots to rot.

Ornithogalum

(Chincherinchee, Star of Bethlehem)

This flower is made up of hundreds of tiny star-shaped white flowers coming from the top of the stem. The flowers are green on the outside, and during dull weather, they close to display the green exteriors of their petals.

AVAILABILITY
Summer

CONDITIONING TIPS
This flower needs only a fresh cut and clean water. The star of Bethlehem will last several weeks with clean water.

FASCINATING FACTS
The genus name *Ornithogalum* is derived from the Greek words *ornithos* (bird) and *gala* (milk) in reference to the white color of the flowers. In Greek, the phrase *bird's milk* was used to describe something amazing. These beautiful flowers are great in bouquets. The star of Bethlehem is often used in Christian ceremonies, such as marriages, christenings, and baptisms.

Pampas Grass (*Cortaderia selloana*)

Pampas grass is the flower of a variety of grass that is typically used dry. It is silky and sheddy, making it a treat for designers looking to create movement in their arrangement.

AVAILABILITY
All year

CONDITIONING TIPS
This grass sheds terribly, as in nature the feathery seeds are readily dispersed by the wind. Designers will typically spray it with hairspray before using it to keep the bits from getting everywhere. Remember, it is easier to continue to cut the grass down if it is too tall, but once cut, it's impossible to make it taller. Lifespan in a vase is almost forever.

FASCINATING FACTS
There are many grasses that flower; however, all that are tall and used by designers are called pampas grass, even though they may actually be a different grass. Pampas grass is great for tablescapes and for adding neutral tones to a fall flower arrangement.

Peony (*Paeonia* spp.)

Peonies, known for their fragrant, old-fashioned blossoms, are a classic. The exquisite, sweetly aromatic blossoms come in a variety of single and double flowers in white, pink, rose, and deep crimson. Peonies' layered blossoms can reach up to 10 inches wide and are a favorite of both gardeners and florists.

AVAILABILITY
Late April to mid-June

CONDITIONING TIPS
Sweet peony nectar is a favorite of ants, so be sure to shake off any that are crawling on the buds. Ideally, purchase when buds are just starting to open. They can be cut or purchased fully open, but will only be stunning for a few days. Cut the lower leaves off and any leaves that will be beneath the waterline. Put them in lukewarm water and keep them out of direct sunlight. Change the water every couple days.

FASCINATING FACTS
In addition to their stunning beauty and sweet fragrance, peonies are a favorite of brides because they represent love and romance and are considered a good omen for a happy marriage. Lighter pink peonies are the most fragrant. A garden peony can still produce flowers after more than 100 years.

Peony, Coral Charm

The coral charm peony is one of the most beloved peony varieties. It is a double peony (meaning that it has multiple rows of petals), and it has the amazing ability to not only change size but also color. This peony starts out fuchsia, then fades to pink before turning white when it is fully open. Finally, in one last flair of life, it changes to yellow.

AVAILABILITY
Mid-spring

CONDITIONING TIPS
To get these peonies to open, give them a fresh cut and place them in hot water. A spritz of water on the individual flower head will remove any sweet sugar on the flowers and help them open. Placing the hard heads under the nozzle of a clothing steamer will get them to pop open even faster as the flower petals expand.

FASCINATING FACTS
Most florists store these dry, still in their box and set on their side in a cooler, for up to two weeks. This will prevent the flower from opening up and beginning its bloom cycle. To extend their lives, as with all peonies, you can give them a fresh cut, place the stems in cold water, and set them back in a cooler. This will slow their cycle down to a crawl.

Peony, Tree
(*Paeonia* sect. *Moutan*)

Tree peonies are shrubby and have permanent woody stems. Tree peonies have much larger single-petaled flowers than their cousins boom peony and standard peony. These are much more delicate and much more expensive.

AVAILABILITY
Spring

CONDITIONING TIPS
This flower is best cut while still in bud form. If the flower is open, it is important to take great care, as it is very delicate. A long cut with a knife and placing it in a vase with hot water will get these beauties to pop open.

FASCINATING FACTS
The Netherlands produces about 50 million peony stems a year.

Phlox

Phlox is prized for its showy, trumpet-shaped flowers with five petals, which bloom in clusters along the stems. Phlox comes in white, pink, purple, red, and blue.

AVAILABILITY
Summer to early fall

CONDITIONING TIPS
Phlox is considered one of the greatest filler flowers on the market. The long, sturdy stems are easy to arrange in a vase and can provide support for weaker stems like dahlias and lilies. Phlox should be cut when the flowers are fully open, and it will last a long time while keeping its shape. Remove all the foliage and place in warm water after giving the stem a long cut with a knife.

FASCINATING FACTS
The name phlox is derived from the Greek word *phlego*, meaning flame, which refers to the radiant luminosity of the flowers.

Poppy, Iceland
(*Papaver nudicaule*)

Iceland poppies' translucent flowers sit on the end of long, hairy stems, which can range in height from 6 to 24 inches. The bowl-shaped flowers of Iceland poppies have a crepe-paper texture and come in bright and pastel shades of white, pink, red, orange, and yellow—but they are not limited to single colors. The blue-green hairy foliage is at the base of the plant.

AVAILABILITY

Summer

CONDITIONING TIPS

Look for buds that are just beginning to open and show a bit of color. Sear the ends of the stems with a candle flame or plunge them into boiling water for a few seconds before arranging in cold water. As a cut flower, the Iceland poppy is one of the longest-lasting poppies, but it doesn't tolerate heat as well as other poppies. Vase life is around 5 to 7 days.

FASCINATING FACTS

Poppies have been grown as ornamental plants since 5000 BCE in Mesopotamia. Not all poppies contain opium, but all poppies are poisonous and can affect the central nervous system in mammals.

Poppy Pods (*Papaver* spp.)

The pod of the poppy flower is what's left on the stem once the flower blooms and the petals fall away. Each seed pod can hold more than two hundred seeds, which naturally shake out through the tiny slits on the pod.

AVAILABILITY

Late spring, after the poppies have bloomed out

CONDITIONING TIPS

Purchasing dried poppy pods is legal; it's when you try to extract opium from them that things get dicey. Poppy pods are amazing in arrangements, both for adding flair and as a filler. Simply cut the pod and put the stem in a tiny bit of treated water so that the stem doesn't rot.

FASCINATING FACTS

If you've ever ordered bagels, you're familiar with poppy seeds. This is where they come from.

Protea, Blushing Bride (*Serruria florida*)

This is a miniature version of the crown proteas and is often in spray form with one to more than eight nodding flower heads per stem. It's show-stopping papery texture gives it a fascinating look. Its white bracts are flushed with pink and surround a central fluffy mass of delicate florets. They can range from three to ten or more blooms per stem.

AVAILABILITY
Late summer

CONDITIONING TIPS
The blushing bride is delicate and sometimes unpredictable. Put the flower in hot water, and then keep it in a cool place to extend vase life.

FASCINATING FACTS
Some say that *blushing bride* refers to a bride who is a virgin and nervous about her wedding night. Others say the name is derived from the resemblance of the flower to a bridal gown. Whatever the case, more and more brides are picking this head-turner for their walk down the aisle.

Protea, Crown (*Protea* spp.)

(King Protea, Queen Protea, Honey Pot, Flowering Sugar Bush)

These proteas, and others in the family, are the largest novelties of their kind. They range from 6 to 7 inches long and 6 to 10 inches wide.

AVAILABILITY
Summer

CONDITIONING TIPS
These desert flowers don't take much work; however, their foliage dries out quickly, so it is best to give them a spray.

FASCINATING FACTS
The King Protea is South Africa's national flower, and its dormant buds can survive wildfires. After fires in the dry Cape land, the King Protea often rises.

Protea, Pincushion (*Leucospermum* spp.)

(Pincushion)

Pincushion proteas resemble small pincushions used in sewing. The flower is rounded, compact, and colorful. They typically come in rich, eye-popping orange and yellow colors.

AVAILABILITY
Summer

CONDITIONING TIPS
Pincushion proteas add wonderful texture and vibrant color to arrangements. Sometimes it takes just one to make a bold floral statement. Simply cut and put in water.

FASCINATING FACTS
If you think they look rather alien, consider that proteas are considered to be one of the oldest plants on earth, dating back 300 million years to the ancient supercontinent Gondwanaland.

Queen Anne's Lace (*Daucus carota*)

(Wild Carrot)

This field flower, also known as the flower of the carrot, has won the hearts of so many due to its fragile, lacelike appearance. While it looks delicate, it is actually a very prolific wild field flower.

AVAILABILITY
Mid-summer to early fall

CONDITIONING TIPS
Separate each floret from the stem that yields a flower. With a floral knife, give each stem a long, angled cut, and place in a vase of hot water with plenty of antibacterials. Spritz the top with water and place the vase in the cooler.

FASCINATING FACTS
The flower of Queen Anne's lace will begin to shrink late in the season, curl up, and become a tumbleweed. That could be a reason why it is so prolific in fields across the globe.

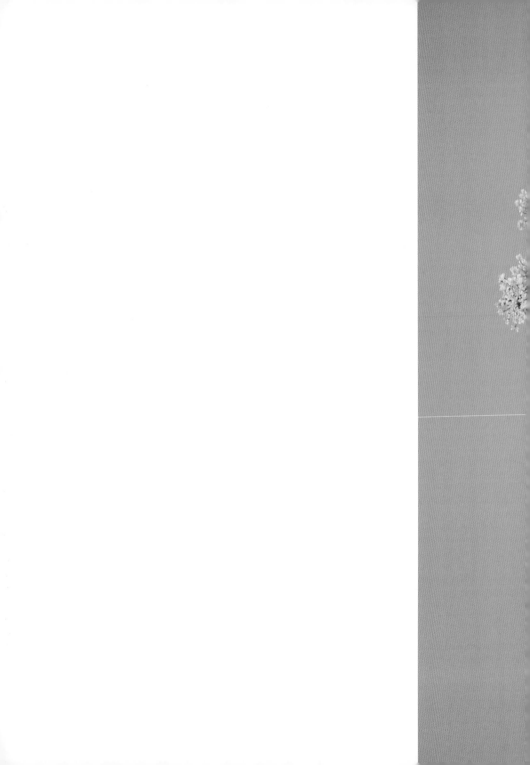

Ranunculus, Buttercup

These beauties range in size and color, but not by much—they're generally 1 to 2 inches across. Buttercups are considered to be "simple" because the floral parts—petals, sepals, stamens, and pistils—are all separate from one another and of an indefinite number.

AVAILABILITY
Late winter through spring

CONDITIONING TIPS
As with other ranunculus, remove all the foliage and take off any extra buds and put them in a separate vase. It's best to wear gloves when working with ranunculus, as it contains toxins, and excessive handling can cause contact dermatitis in humans.

FASCINATING FACTS
This was the *it* flower for a period in the 2000s because of its ability to generate a whimsical flowing look for flower arrangements.

Ranunculus, Butterfly

The butterfly ranunculus has a limited petal count, like the anemone, on a wiry stem. The flower petals have a waxy sheen, which catches the light and gives them a sparkle, like a butterfly's wing, which helps boost their life. Each stem can carry up to a dozen flowers and makes them perfect for achieving a whimsical look.

AVAILABILITY
Spring

CONDITIONING TIPS
Remove all the foliage; however, unlike the buttercup ranunculus, it is best to keep the stems whole until you know if you need to edit them down to single stems. The butterfly ranunculus has a surprisingly long life; just remove the spent blossoms, and the other buds will carry on in a continuous fountain of flowers. With proper care, vase life is up to 14 days.

FASCINATING FACTS
Butterfly ranunculus was invented by a Japanese breeder and has quickly gained popularity around the world. Unlike the older styles of ranunculus we've been familiar with, the butterfly variety comes with a minimal number of petals and fits in perfectly in Bohemian as well as rustic-looking floral designs.

Ranunculus, Clooney Hanoi

(Clooney Hanoi)

Clooney Hanoi ranunculuses are very similar to their cousin, the buttercup ranunculus, except the shape, size, angles, and number of flower petals are different. Clooney Hanoi flaunts soft pink and white blooms, which are long lasting and as stunning as peonies and roses. When it opens fully, a green eye at the center is revealed.

AVAILABILITY
Late winter through spring

CONDITIONING TIPS
Remove all the foliage from these beauties as well as any unopened buds that are attached. After removing the buds, keep them in a separate container of water, as they will sometimes continue to grow and blossom. The Clooney Hanoi has an extremely high petal count and tends to open in a magnificent fashion once put in water. Considering the delicate nature of the blooms, they are curiously long lasting.

FASCINATING FACTS
The Clooney Hanoi is grown in Italy. The lush blooms are truly stunning, which have made this a very popular wedding flower.

Rhododendron

Rhododendrons are cultivated for their beautiful, fragrant flowers and ornamental leaves, which are arranged in a spiral shape along the stems. The flowers, which have a trumpet shape, are available in several colors, including white, pink, purple, red, and orange.

AVAILABILITY
Late spring

CONDITIONING TIPS
Cut the rhododendron stem to the desired length and place it immediately in warm (approximately 100°F) water with a few drops of bleach. To keep the blooms looking good for as long as possible, change the water every few days and give the stem a fresh cut each time. They will last in a vase from 5 to 10 days.

FASCINATING FACTS
The word *rhododendron* comes from two ancient Greek words: *rhodon* (rose) and *dendron* (tree). Big news for those ancient Greeks: rhododendrons grow as evergreen and deciduous shrubs.

Rose, Garden (*Rosa* spp.)

The rose is the flower of love and one of the most popular flowering plants in the world. Their flowers vary in size, shape, and color, running from white to yellows and reds. Rose thorns are actually prickles, outgrowths of the stem's epidermis. A rose's elegance and silky petals are hard to beat, and their fragrance is an ultimate luxury. Some describe the smell as that of black China tea with hints of sun-drenched citrus.

AVAILABILITY
All year

CONDITIONING TIPS
Remove all of the foliage, cut the stems on a sharp angle, and place them in hot water immediately. If you are hoping to get your roses to open extra bright, you can either blow the blooms open or spin the stem like a pellet drum to open the flower head. Due to the delicate nature of most garden roses, they will typically last 3 to 4 days rather than the 7 days that hybrid tea roses typically last.

FASCINATING FACTS
According to Guinness World Records, roses are the oldest species of plant to be grown as decoration. The ancient Romans grew the flowers in vast plantations and used them to decorate buildings and people, while the petals were often sprinkled to create elegant carpets. In 1986, President Ronald Reagan stood in the famous White House Rose Garden and officially made the rose the national flower of the United States.

Rose, Hybrid Tea (*Rosa* spp.)

Hybrid tea roses are considered rose royalty and one of the oldest classes of roses. Known for their long, elegant, pointed buds, one per stem, hybrid tea roses have been cultivated in almost every color, including lavender, pink, peach, white, yellow, and red—just not blue. The lightly fragrant blooms have a fruity scent and many petals, which open slowly.

AVAILABILITY
All year

CONDITIONING TIPS
Remove all of the foliage, cut the stems on a sharp angle, and place them in hot water immediately. If you are hoping to get your roses to open extra bright, you can either blow the blooms open or spin the stem like a pellet drum to open the flower head. When conditioned well, this flower should last 5 to 7 days.

FASCINATING FACTS
The hybrid tea rose is the most popular Valentine's Day flower and comes in many varieties, including the lipstick red "Christian Dior," the ivory and pink "Diana, Princess of Wales," the deep yellow "Henry Fonda," and the apricot-colored "Marilyn Monroe."

Rose, Spray (*Rosa* spp.)

(Sweetheart Rose, Miniature Rose)

Spray roses are miniature standard roses that have multiple petite blooms per stem. They come in a vast array of colors and often contain roses in various stages of maturity, from tight buds to fully open blooms. Spray roses are great as accent flowers or bunched together in a larger arrangement and add a touch of romance to any room.

AVAILABILITY
All year

CONDITIONING TIPS
Remove all of the foliage, cut the stems on a sharp angle, and place them in hot water immediately. If you are hoping to get your roses to open extra bright, you can encourage the blooms to open by gently blowing on them as you would the ear of a lover.

FASCINATING FACTS
In the language of flowers, rose colors have different meanings. Red means romantic love. Pink means gratitude. Yellow means get well or friendship. Lavender means love at first sight and enchantment.

Ruscus

(Box Holly, Butcher's Broom)

Ruscus has red berries and a glossy, pointed elegance. This is perhaps the most popular foliage in the floral industry, as it mixes well with most flowers and lasts for a while without water, making it a favorite for use in installations and as wedding greenery.

AVAILABILITY
All year

CONDITIONING TIPS
The life of ruscus can be extended anywhere from two weeks to six months if the recut stems are submerged in plain tap water, or in water that has been treated with a few drops of household bleach and replaced once a week. Pro tip: use both Israeli ruscus and Italian ruscus together to generate a more "wild" look.

FASCINATING FACTS
Ruscus has been used for centuries by butchers as a way to clean their cutting boards. Julius Caesar is thought to have worn ruscus rather than laurel to adorn his head.

Sandersonia
(*Sandersonia aurantiaca*)

(Chinese Lantern, Christmas Bells)

Sandersonia gets its common name from its flowers, which are bell shaped, like thimble-sized lanterns. It has a thin stem and long, slim leaves, which hold up well. Their eye-catching blooms are orange-yellow and look best on their own.

AVAILABILITY
Mid-summer

CONDITIONING TIPS
Remove any unsightly foliage and cut with a sharp knife. This flower does best in cold water.

FASCINATING FACTS
The genus got its name after the Scottish journalist and amateur botanist John Sanderson, who "discovered" the plant in 1851 in South Africa. Sandersonia blooms around Christmastime in South Africa, hence the common name Christmas bells.

Sarracenia

(Pitcher Plant)

A strange, exotic, almost alien-looking plant, the pitcher plant is a carnivorous plant with hollow tubular leaves, which can take the form of a trumpet or an urn and allow the plant to "eat" insects. Many different plants are known as pitcher plants, but the most common in the cut flower world is the sarracenia.

AVAILABILITY
Summer through fall

CONDITIONING TIPS
These flowers attract and capture all sorts of insects. Be cautious when cutting these flowers to length, as there are always a few bugs still in the pitcher. To keep the pitcher plant from caving in on itself, cut it with a knife, place it in warm water, and mist with a spray bottle.

FASCINATING FACTS
Sarracenias are starting to become much more common as houseplants. If you decide you like the look of them, you might get the bug to get one.

Scabiosa

(Pincushion Flower)

Scabiosas include several varieties and hundreds of colors. All include a small beautiful bloom atop a long skinny stem. They are perfect flowers for whimsical and rustic-style flower arrangements.

AVAILABILITY
Summer

CONDITIONING TIPS
These flowers can often come with a straw around the neck of the flower stem to keep the delicate flower from breaking. This is perfectly safe for the flower, but it can be removed if it doesn't look good. Vase life is rather short. Put them in warm water, and they'll last 4 or 5 days.

FASCINATING FACTS
The name scabiosa comes from the Latin word *scabere*, which means to "scratch." The Romans used to use the plant to treat scabies, a highly contagious skin infestation.

Snapdragon
(*Antirrhinum* spp.)

(Dragon Flower, Dog Flower)

Snapdragons are tall spikes consisting of ten to thirty beautiful snout-shaped blooms along the stem. These flowers, which resemble the face and mouth of a dragon, can come in variations of pink, purple, lavender, burgundy, orange, white, and yellow.

AVAILABILITY
Spring and summer

CONDITIONING TIPS
Choose sturdy, straight spikes with buds showing color and one-third to one-half of the flowers open. Remove all the foliage. The snapdragon is one of the unusual summer flowers for which cold water is much better for longevity than warm or hot water. Snapdragons are susceptible to ethylene gas, so keep them away from ripe fruits and vegetables.

FASCINATING FACTS
The dry seed pods of the flowers resemble miniature skulls. Perhaps this is why snapdragons were thought to offer protection from both witchcraft and aging.

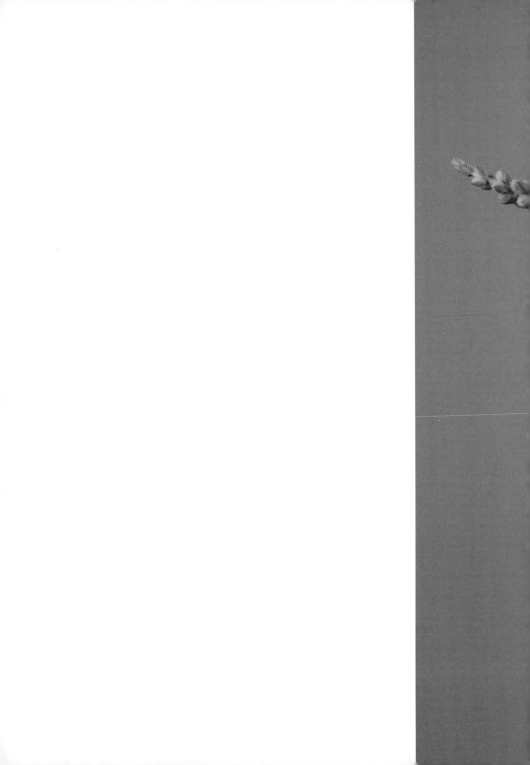

Snowberry (*Symphoricarpos*)

(Ghostberry, Pinkberry, Waxberry)

Snowberry is a shrub that is part of the honeysuckle family. The berries, which appear all the way up the outer stems of the plant, are often found in shades of white or pink. While the berry may look delicious, it is mildly toxic, and you and your pets should not eat it.

AVAILABILITY
Mid-autumn

CONDITIONING TIPS
Snowberry grows on a woody stem, and smashing the stem is good for water absorption. Often, the leaves are the first to brown and wilt, so it is best to remove them as soon as possible.

FASCINATING FACTS
In the past, branches of snowberry have been used for a variety of purposes, including as broom bristles and as arrow shafts. Due to the foaming properties of this plant, some Native American tribes used the fruit of the snowberry as a natural shampoo.

Solidago

(Goldenrod)

Unless it is otherwise tinted, this amazing flower only comes in yellow. Solidago is the cut flower that most closely resembles a meadow flower from the prairie, and it is best used in rustic-style flower arrangements.

AVAILABILITY
Summer

CONDITIONING TIPS
Remove all the foliage and put the stems in warm water to help open the flowers. With its vivid color and ample texture, solidago adds some knockout to any arrangement.

FASCINATING FACTS
In the 1920s, Thomas Edison, Henry Ford, and Harvey Firestone tried to use the concentration of latex on the leaves of solidago in the production of rubber. Ford's first Model T automobile used rubber made from solidago foliage.

Statice (*Limonium* spp.)

(Sea Lavender, Limonium)

Clumps of long-lasting, brightly colored, papery flowers cluster at the end of statice's long, sturdy stems. It comes mainly in shades of purple and blue, but is also available in white, yellow, peach, pink, and rose.

AVAILABILITY
All year

CONDITIONING TIPS
There is almost no need to condition this flower, as it will dry in the same state as when the flower is fresh. Vase life is up to 14 days. Hung upside down in bunches, statice makes a dried flower that will last for years.

FASCINATING FACTS
In the language of flowers, statice is associated with memory and remembrance. Perhaps this is because the flower holds its color for a long time when dried. Put it in as a filler to say "I miss you."

Stock
(*Matthiola incana*)

(Gillyflower)

Even though it doesn't have the most exciting name, stock is a beautiful, spiky stem with large, closely arranged flowers. It flowers from top to bottom. The scent is spicy and clove-like. Stocks come in a wide range of colors, including white, cream, pink, apricot, magenta, red, purple, yellow, and green.

AVAILABILITY
All year

CONDITIONING TIPS
Stock stems are dense, which makes water intake difficult. To lengthen vase life, recut the stems and cut away any thick, white fibrous base. Place immediately in cool water with a drop of bleach. Change the water often and recut the stems. Vase life is around 7 days.

FASCINATING FACTS
Stock is actually a member of the cabbage family. It has edible flowers and green seed pods, which have a radish-like flavor and are good in salads and as garnishes.

Strawflower (*Xerochrysum bracteatum*)

(Golden Everlasting, Paper Daisy)

Strawflowers are similar to asters in shape but smaller, and like daisies, the center is made up of a cluster of tiny individual flowers. The surrounding petals are actually bracts that feel like waxed paper. Strawflowers come in a wide range of colors, including white, yellow, pink, and red.

AVAILABILITY
Summer

CONDITIONING TIPS
Strawflowers are known to have very heavy heads and weak stems. Most florists will stick a wire up the center of the stem to help keep them upright. Remove all the foliage. Cut flowers can last 14 to 21 days in a vase. When dried, the flowers will retain their color for a long time, but don't let the "everlasting" moniker fool you—they will fade and become brittle as they age.

FASCINATING FACTS
This is a popular flower for the world-renowned Pasadena Tournament of Roses Parade. In order to make the color and flower petals go further, the flower heads are put through a blender; when they're making parade floats, they want to use the flower as a colorful material (like wallpaper) rather than as a bloom.

Sunflower, Common Green or Brown (*Helianthus* spp.)

The blossom of the sunflower is called a head. As many as two thousand flowers can make up one sunflower bloom. The yellow petals on the outside of the bloom are called ray florets. The fuzzy brown centers are called disc florets, and this is where the seeds develop.

AVAILABILITY
Mid-summer through early fall

CONDITIONING TIPS
Cut the stem at a 45-degree angle, leaving at least 24 inches of stem. Place the flowers in hot water immediately after cutting and let the flowers sit in indirect light for a few hours.

FASCINATING FACTS
Even though sunflowers are native to North America, the Guinness World Records says the tallest sunflower was grown in Germany and measured 30 feet, 1 inch. Yellow is the most common color, but there are also red, orange, and purple sunflowers.

Sunflower, Teddy Bear (*Helianthus annuus*)

Like their name implies, teddy bear sunflowers are cute and fluffy with a fuzzy center, and therefore no seeds. This American heirloom sunflower variety is known for its small height and its cheery yellow pom-pom-like flowers. There can be as many as five flowers per stalk.

AVAILABILITY
Mid-summer to October

CONDITIONING TIPS
The flowers should be harvested just before the bloom is fully open. They have a vase life of around 7 days.

FASCINATING FACTS
Dutch impressionist painter Vincent van Gogh was obsessed with sunflowers. His iconic paintings of teddy bear sunflowers have sold for millions of dollars at auction.

Sweet Pea
(*Lathyrus odoratus*)

There might not be a cuter flower than the sweet pea. With perfumed blooms that resemble fringed butterflies in a rainbow of colors and slender stems that appear to be folded, the sweet pea vine makes an incredible cut flower.

AVAILABILITY

Spring

CONDITIONING TIPS

For the longest vase life, pick stems that have at least two unopened flowers at the tip. The stems must be cut with a knife, at an angle, and placed into a vase of clean water. Too much water will cause the flower to wilt early, so be sure to have only 2 to 3 inches of water in the vase and do not spritz the flowers. They last 4 or 5 days in a vase.

FASCINATING FACTS

Sweet peas are native to Italy. A seventeenth-century Sicilian monk sent sweet pea seeds to England, and the genus became all the rage in the Victorian era. Want another reason to love them? Although we love sweet peas' heavenly scent, it's bothersome to flies and thus helps keep them at bay.

Tansy (*Tanacetum* spp.)

(Golden Buttons, Bitter Buttons)

The bright yellow flowers of the tansy look like buttons on clothes and grow in flat-topped clusters. The leaves are feathery and fernlike and have a pungent camphor-like odor when crushed. The plant can grow from 1 to 5 feet tall, and it has been listed as a noxious weed in many parts of the United States.

AVAILABILITY
August and September

CONDITIONING TIPS
Wear gloves and long sleeves when handling the tansy, as it contains an oil known as thujone, which may cause skin irritation or contact dermatitis.

FASCINATING FACTS
Even though tansy has been used historically for medical purposes, from digestive ailments to treating jaundice, its potent chemical thujone is toxic and can cause convulsions or death in horses, cows, and humans if eaten in excess.

Tulips, Parrot (*Tulipa* spp.)

Gorgeously exotic-looking parrot tulips have ruffled and sometimes twisted petals that come in a breathtaking array of colors that evoke the bright hues of parrot feathers. These wild shapes and colors aren't the result of people trying to create them. They are their own incredible gifts from nature, spontaneous mutations in the genes of ordinary tulips.

AVAILABILITY
January to May

CONDITIONING TIPS
Tulips should be cut when the color first shows on the bloom, or cracking, as it's called. Remove all the foliage, except maybe one leaf for style, and cone the bunch to ensure it doesn't droop. Allow them to fully open in the vase. To prolong their beauty, keep them away from direct sunlight and supply lots of water regularly. Tulips last around 5 days.

FASCINATING FACTS
In the 1600s, parrot tulips were all the rage. Artist after artist featured a single subject in their paintings: the parrot tulip, each itself a stunning work of art.

Tulip, Standard (*Tulipa* spp.)

Tulips are amazing flowers with a defining shape and a spectrum of stunning colors. They continue to grow—some as much as 7 inches—and become even more beautiful throughout their vase life. Although red varieties remain the most popular, colors range from white to violet to pale yellow to deep mahogany.

AVAILABILITY
All year

CONDITIONING TIPS
Tulips actually continue to grow after they are cut, bending and twisting toward the light. We call that "walking" in the vase. If tulips are well watered and kept away from heat, they will last from 7 to 10 days.

FASCINATING FACTS
Tulipa is the Latin word for tulip, derived from *tulipan*, which means "turban," so named because of a tulip's shape. When we think of tulips, we all think of Holland. Even though Holland is the largest producer of tulips, the flower actually originated in Turkey, where they grow in the wild. They were brought to Holland in the late 1500s via Great Britain.

Tweedia (*Oxypetalum coeruleum*)

(Blue Milkweed)

The tweedia flower comes from a tropical milkweed vine native to Brazil. The pale blue or sometimes white or pink bloom is small and star-shaped, with five petals. The flower is rustic and adds a romantic, soft, wispy feel to designs. It goes well in field flower arrangements.

AVAILABILITY
Summer

CONDITIONING TIPS
Tweedia is a great cut flower, lasting 5 to 10 days in a vase. When removing the leaves from this flower's stem, you will immediately see a white secretion that is synonymous with the milkweeds. Beware: this secretion is an irritant to some humans and animals. You might want to wear gloves when working with it.

FASCINATING FACTS
Many Bohemian brides are now wearing tweedia flowers in their hair for a romantic, vintage look.

Veronica

(Speedwell, Bird's Eye, Gypsyweed)

The veronica flower grows straight up out of a bush that is known for its spikes of flowers that come in white, blue, pink, and purple. The flower itself is a cone of hundreds of mini flowers. Veronica has a whimsical movement and is perfect for designs that evoke flowering gardens.

AVAILABILITY
Summer

CONDITIONING TIPS
Remove as much foliage as possible, give the stems a fresh angular cut, and place them in warm water. These flowers also enjoy a spritz. The name speedwell might come from veronica's propensity to start dropping petals after just a few days.

FASCINATING FACTS
In Ireland, veronica spikes are pinned to clothes to keep travelers safe from trouble.

Viburnum

(Snowball)

There are seventy different varieties of viburnum, but only ten are used regularly in the cut flower industry. The snowball viburnum is a chartreuse flower with big ball-shaped blooms and large tri-pointed leaves.

AVAILABILITY
Early spring

CONDITIONING TIPS
All foliage must be removed by twisting the leaves from the stems. Then, the wood stem should be smashed and the casing scraped off.

FASCINATING FACTS
The Dutch have long been the most talented and prolific at cultivating this variety. It takes 2 years for each plant to produce a flower worthy of exporting.

Wax Flower
(*Chamelaucium* spp.)

Wax flower is a lovely evergreen shrub with delicate branches and
sweet, fragrant blooms. The colors of wax flowers range from dark pink
to creamy white. They give fine texture to a garden arrangement or a
wedding bouquet.

AVAILABILITY
Late spring through summer

CONDITIONING TIPS
Separate the stems into usable pieces and remove the pine-like needles.
After giving the woody stem a fresh cut, place it in hot water.

FASCINATING FACTS
When the needlelike leaves are pulled from the stems of wax flowers, the
fragrance is a fresh, clean lemony scent.

Winterberry (*Ilex verticallata*)

(Fever Bush)

Ilex is a species of flowering plants in the holly family with branching stems that bountifully bear colorful berries in yellow, orange, and red. Winterberry is a deciduous holly, which means it sheds its leaves in the fall. The vibrant berries are the main show.

AVAILABILITY
October to January

CONDITIONING TIPS
Winterberry branches don't require much care. They can last 1 to 2 weeks, and if dried, they can last even longer.

FASCINATING FACTS
Winterberry is super popular around the Christmas holidays. It's a terrific sturdy filler and combines well with other flowers and branches.

Yarrow
(*Achillea millefolium*)

(Milfoil)

Each stem of yarrow has multiple flat flower heads covered in tiny daisy-like flowers that can be white, reddish, or pink. Yarrow has dense fernlike foliage of fine feathery leaves spirally arranged on a stem, which has given yarrow its common name, milfoil, meaning a thousand leaves.

AVAILABILITY
Summer

CONDITIONING TIPS
Yarrow is a long-lasting cut flower and combines well with romantic flowers as well as those with bolder shapes and textures. Yarrows can also be dried by simply leaving them in a vase without water.

FASCINATING FACTS
Yarrow has been called the poor man's pepper because it has a bitter and pungent taste. If a cow eats too much yarrow while grazing, the cow's milk will become bitter.

Zinnia

These brightly colored flowers bloom from a bushy brush plant belonging to the aster family. Flowers vary in size, from 1 to 7 inches, and in form—they might have single, semi-double, or double layered petals. Zinnias come in a wide range of bright colors, including red, purple, lilac, white, yellow, and orange.

AVAILABILITY
Summer

CONDITIONING TIPS
Zinnias last much better when kept in cold water—and not too much, because when the stems are submerged, they tend to rot quickly. Just 2 to 3 inches in the vase will be fine, and change the water often, or you will end up with a pile of swampy plant matter. They'll last at least 7 days in a vase before starting to look tired.

FASCINATING FACTS
Native to the American Southwest and Mexico, zinnias were once considered small and ugly. When the Spanish first saw the flower in Mexico, they named it *mal de ojos*, or sickness of the eye. When zinnias were then introduced to Europeans, they became known as poorhouse flowers because they were so common and easy to grow. Don't let that stop you. Zinnias are one of those flowers that florists love the most because they are abundant and hold up very well in the summer. They are best used in rustic-style flower arrangements.

Acknowledgments

If you are lucky enough to get the privilege to become a florist, you will realize that there are so many moving parts that need to come together in order to do it well. We would like to thank all of the FlowerSchool community for their support and dedication to learning. However, there are certain individuals that, without their support, this book would not have been possible.

I am lucky enough to be acquainted with one of the world's best writers, Bruce Littlefield. Without Bruce's talent and absolute LOVE of flowers, we would not have been able to make this the amazing reference book it is. Thank you, Bruce.

We are blessed with amazing staff, both past and present, who I can't thank enough. Brittany Lenig, Tara Sandonato, Thomas Sebanius, and Jessi Owen are at the core of FlowerSchool and its mission. Thank you to the ends of the earth for your support. Meredith Perez of Belle Fleur, Juan Villanueva of Villanueva Designs, and Paulina Nieliwocki of Blue Jasmine Floral. Thank you for your support and continuing to carry the torch. Our instructors Meghan Riley, Jin Park, Barbara Mele, Elena Mencarelli, and Sharon Prendergast. Our current roster of masters, Victoria Ahn of Designs By Ahn, LaParis Phillips of Brooklyn Blooms, Kelsea Olivia of East Olivia, Olivier Giugni, Ingrid Carozzi of Tin Can Studios, Claudia Hanlin of The Wedding Library, Emily Pinon, Jean-Pascal Lemire, Atsushi Taniguchi of Jardin du l'Ilony, Kiana Underwood of Tulipina, and Remco Van Vliet. Thank you for being open to sharing with such passion. And thank you to the incomparable Elizabeth Armstrong Brown: you are truly everything.

Finding all these flowers to photograph is no small feat. We could not have done this without the generous support and help of Michael and Joe at FleuraMetz, Vinney and Ed at New York Flower Group, formally Dutch Flower Line, and the lovely folks at Hilverda de Boer: Bas and Marco. Thank you.

Index

Illustrations are indicated in **BOLD**

dusty miller (*Jacobaea maritima*) (silver dust, silver ragwort, maritime ragwort), 100, **101**
dysentery, 196

E

echinacea (coneflower), 102, **103**
edible flowers, 44, 52, 62, 114, 152, 308
Edison, Thomas, 304
enchantment, 286
England, Victorian, 24, 318
enthusiasm, 36
eremurus (foxtail lily, desert candle), 104, **105**
eryngium (sea holly, blue thistle), 106, **107**, **108**, **109**
eternal youth, 4
eucalyptus, 110, **111**
evil spirits, 148, 166
eye diseases, 88

F

fairies, 28
fall availability, 6, 12, 18, 34, 36, 38, 58, 62, 68, 74, 80, 82, 84, 90, 102, 132, 136, 142, 148, 160, 162, 164, 192, 204, 218, 222, 250, 266, 292, 312, 316, 322
fatigue, 40
fennel, 40
fern, 112, **113**
fevers, 40, 78. 90, 110
"fifth element," 4
Firestone, Harvey, 304
fleur-de-lis, 172
florist knife and clipper, xvi
florist supplies, xvi
florist tricks, x
flowers in art, 316, 324
foliage, xi, xvi
Ford, Henry, 304
forsythia (golden bells), 114, **115**
freesia, 116, **117**
friendship, 8, 286

fritillaria (checkered lily, fox's grape), 118, **119**, **120**, **121**
fritillaria, Crown Imperial (*Fritillaria imperialis*), 122, **123**, **124**, **125**

G

gala (milk), 238
Germany, 312
get well, 286
gin, 168
ginger (*Etlingera elatior*) (torch ginger, ginger lily), 126, **127**
gladiators, Roman, 128
gladiolus (sword lily), 128, **129**, **130**, **131**
gloriosa lily (*Gloriosa* spp.) (fire lily, flame lily, creeping lily, cat's claw), 132, **133**, **134**, **135**
gomphrena (globe amaranth), 136, **137**
Gondwanaland, 264
good fortune, 6
grapes, xvii
grasses, xvii, 240
gratitude, 286
Great Britain, 326
Greek, 228, 238, 250, 278
Guatemala, 84
Guernsey island, 192
Guinness World Records, 280, 312
gypsophila (baby's breath, soap root, chalk plant), 138, **139**, **140**, **141**

H

hanami "Watching blossoms," 56
happiness, 20, 60
hedera (ivy), 142, **143**
heliconia (lobster claw, wild plantain, bird of paradise), 144, **145**
helleborus (hellebore, Lenten rose), 145, 146
herbal medicine, 106, 196, 204, 216, 322
Himalayan Mountains, 226
Hindu philosophy, 230
Hippocrates, 166
Holland. *See* Netherlands.

About the Authors

CALVERT CRARY is Executive Director of FlowerSchool New York and author of *Flower School*. After working for over a decade as a professional photographer, Calvert made the transition to floral entrepreneur in 2006. Since then, he has trained and coached many students, teaching them how to open their own flower shops and reorganize existing floral businesses into thriving careers.

BRUCE LITTLEFIELD is a best-selling author, lifestyle expert, and arbiter of American fun. Hailed as a "lifestyle authority" by the *New York Times* and as a "modern-day Erma Bombeck" by NPR, he is a contributor to *Good Morning America* and has appeared on NBC's *Today* show, CBS's *Early Show* and ABC's *The View*, as well as MSNBC, *Rachael Ray*, *The Soup*, and *The Better Show* podcast. He has authored eighteen books, including *Garage Sale America*, *Merry Christmas, America!,* and *Airstream Living*, critically acclaimed adventures in Americana. His *Bedtime Book for Dogs* is the first book written with words dogs understand and kids love to read. He is also the co-author of six *New York Times* bestsellers with well-known personalities, including *Use What You've Got* (with *Shark Tank* mogul Barbara Corcoran), *My Two Moms* (with civil rights advocate Zach Wahls), and *The Sell* (with Bravo star Fredrik Eklund). Follow him @brucelittlefield and visit www.brucelittlefield.com